MOLLUSCS

MOLLUSCS

Text by Václav Pfleger

BLITZ EDITIONS

Text by Václav Pfleger
Translated by Margot Schierlová
Photographs by Jiří Poláček, Dušan Šimánek, Václav Pfleger,
Július Slabecius
Line drawings by Eva Smrčinová and Gordon Riley
Graphic design by Stanislav Seifert

Designed and produced by Aventinum Publishing House, Prague,
Czech Republic
This English edition published 1999 by Blitz Editions,
an imprint of Bookmart Ltd.
Registered Number 2372865
Trading as Bookmart Limited
Desford Road, Enderby, Leicester LE9 5AD

ISBN 1-85605-449-7
Printed in the Czech Republic by Polygrafia, a.s., Prague
3/07/14/51-03

Contents

Introduction

About 1,500 species of land and freshwater gastropods and bivalves occur in Europe but these represent a very small portion of the entire phylum of Mollusca. This photographic guide covers about 10 percent of these 1,500 species and is therefore not a complete key or guide to the entire non-marine molluscan fauna of Europe. It is intended primarily for keen naturalists and it aims to show that even among European molluscs there are many species which have attractive colouring, shell shape or surface sculpture, although they naturally cannot compete with exotic marine shells. Compared with the marine fauna, on which popular literature is available, the identification of land snails is often very difficult, partly because of the small size of most of the shells and partly due to the lack of popular literature accessible to the general public. It is hoped that this book will evoke a serious interest in the study of this somewhat neglected but interesting group of animals.

The species described in the book belong to all 45 European families and come from different parts of the Continent. The members of families containing very small species (6 mm and less) are illustrated only by black-and-white drawings. The photographs are mainly of the larger species and are, if possible, ones which are strikingly coloured and have an interesting shell form or surface sculpture. The accompanying text to every illustrated species includes its zoogeographical range, a general description of the shell, the animal and details of its colour, size, habitat and distribution. Since most of the species are land gastropods, considerable attention is also paid to this group in the introductory text.

Characteristics of molluscs

General features, classification and types of shell

Molluscs — the second largest phylum in the animal kingdom — are characterized by a soft, slimy body and a glandular fold of skin or mantle. The mantle secretes a shell which often gives the mollusc partial or complete shelter for its body. Differences in the shape of the mantle give rise to different types of shells. The phylum Mollusca is divided into a number of classes.

The most primitive molluscan class are the Monoplacophora, with only a few species having a conical or cap-like shell.

The chitons in the class Polyplacophora are also primitive gastropods and they have a shell formed of eight transverse plates or valves.

There is also the curious worm-like class of Aplacophora without a definite shell.

The class Gastropoda contains the most species and the shell of gastropods is made of one part (univalve) and usually coiled into a spiral.

The class Scaphopoda or Tusk Shells have an interesting tubular shell open at both ends.

In the second largest class, the Bivalvia or clams, the two valves of the shell are joined together at the umbones by a hinge, supported by a horny ligament.

The most highly developed molluscs are in the class Cephalopoda, and they do not — apart from minor exceptions — form an external shell, although many of their fossil relatives like the nautilus had one. Cephalopods include octopus, squid and cuttlefish.

Molluscs are a very ancient group of animals, whose origin goes back to the earliest fossil-bearing rocks of the Palaeozoic Era (the Cambrian period, some 500 million years ago). In those days too the seas were full of molluscs, with the result that some extinct (fossil) species are important for estimating the geological age and stratigraphy of the various layers of rock. Molluscs reached the peak of their development in the Caenozoic Era, but even today they are still, numerically, a very large group. The number of species in the phylum varies with the publication. Some authors put it at 120,000, but this figure evidently also includes extinct species and a large number of synonyms which are no longer valid as true species. A common estimate is 80,000 species, the majority of which live in the sea, and about 75 % of this total are gastropods.

The land molluscs described in this book are all gastropods, but the freshwater species include both gastropods and bivalves.

Gastropods (about 50,000—60,000 species) are classified according to the position and type of respiratory organs and divided into the subclasses Prosobranchia, Opisthobranchia and Pulmonata. Whilst there are some land and freshwater prosobranchs, most of the non-marine species in this book are pulmonates. Prosobranchia include freshwater species in which the single gill lies in the mantle cavity in front of the ventricle of the heart; the heart also has only one auricle and there is only one kidney. As their name suggests, the pulmonate gastropods breathe with a 'lung'; this consists of the roof of the mantle cavity, which is protected in a moist pocket and richly supplied with blood vessels which form a capillary network. The whole structure consists of a closed cavity or pocket which opens on to the surface via a small opening on the right side of the body in dextral species. The shell may be normal or reduced to a small plate and is sometimes absent altogether in slugs. Most pulmonates are land animals, but they generally require a damp environment. Species which have reverted to an aquatic mode of life either come to the surface to take air into the 'lung', or have become so thoroughly adapted that they have acquired an accessory respiratory surface and can use oxygen contained in the water.

Bivalves (class Bivalvia or Pelecypoda) comprise some 10,000—20,000 species, about one third of which live in fresh water and the rest in the sea. Bivalves are aquatic animals and breathe by means of gills.

Structure and colouring of the shells

Mollusc shells are composed of several different layers. The thin outer layer or periostracum consists of an organic substance known as conchiolin, whose chemical composition is similar to that of chitin in insects. Below the conchiolin there is a much thicker inorganic layer composed of three layers of crystalline calcium carbonate which was formed on an organic matrix. The innermost layer — nacre, or mother-of-pearl — is best developed in large bivalves like pearl mussels and freshwater mussels; only traces of it are to be seen in other non-marine molluscs.

The many distinguishing features of shells are a study in themselves and some people are only interested in the shell. However, many important features of classification of individual species are found in the anatomy of the body or soft parts, although it is possible to identify many species from the shell alone. When describing the various species, we therefore pay special attention to the morphology or form of the shell (conchological characters).

The degree of hardness and the microstructure of the mollusc shell depend on the manner of its crystallization. The mantle concentrates calcium contained in the blood in given zones along its margin, where it forms crystals of calcium salts in an organic matrix and causes growth at the edge of the shell. The shell material thus formed is influenced by a whole series of factors, including the growth hormones, food, the acidity of the water and the temperature.

The colouring of the shells is produced by organic pigments acquired by the animal from its food. The resultant colours are the outcome of the combination of four basic types of pigments — yellow carotenoids, black melanins, green porphyrins and blue or red indigoids. The basic colour and design are determined genetically in every species (i. e. they are hereditary), although many snails display much variation in colour, which can depend on the environment and food as well. Shell colour sometimes gives camouflage protection from predators.

Most of the groups of pigment-producing cells are localized along the margin of the mantle, at the site of shell growth — in gastropods on the margin of the aperture of the shell, in bivalves along the free ventral edge of the valves. Bright colours also appear in some of the other organs, as well as the shell, e. g. in the foot, the head and the mantle (in slugs).

Morphology of gastropods

The shell

Let us imagine the shell as a tube coiled round a straight line (the axis). Every turn of 360 degrees round the axis gives rise to one twist or whorl. The narrowest, smallest and oldest part of the shell is the apex, which has a pointed tip. From the apex downwards, the shell whorls grow progressively wider, until reaching the aperture or mouth, from which the animal itself protrudes. The shell needs to be observed in three different orientations to see all the diagnostic features: these are shown in the

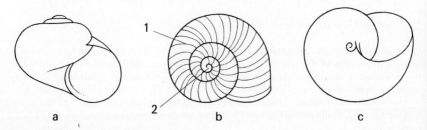

Fig. 1. Main positions of gastropod shell.
a — lateral view, **b** — dorsal view, **c** — ventral view, 1 — growth lines, 2 — protoconch (shell formed by embryo).

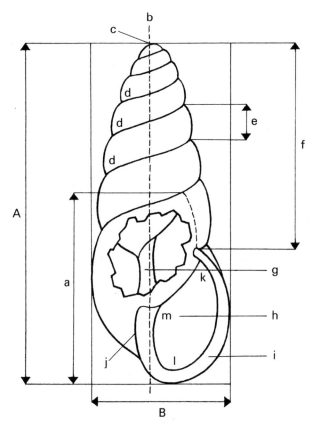

Fig. 2. Main features of a gastropod shell.
A — height, **B** — width, **a** — last (body) whorl, **b** — axis, **c** — apex, **d** — suture, **e** — whorl, **f** — spire, **g** — columella, **h** — aperture, **i** — aperture margin, **j** — position of umbilicus if present, **k**—**l** — outer (palatal) part of aperture, **l**—**m** — columellar part of aperture, **m**—**k** — parietal part of aperture.

diagram (Fig. 1). The dimensions of the shell are determined with the apex of the shell uppermost and the aperture face on. The height is the maximum distance between the tip of the apex and the lowest point of the aperture, measured parallel to the main axis of the shell. The width is the distance — measured perpendicularly to the height that is across the largest whorl at the periphery. Further technical terms will be found in the descriptions of the shells of individual species and in the diagram (Fig. 2).

The line following the contours of the shell with apex uppermost and mouth facing is known as the general outline. It can be straight, convex or occasionally concave. The line following the most tumid parts of the whorls is the circumference

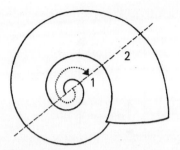

Fig. 3. Determination of number of whorls.

and where the whorls meet is the suture, often a groove seen as a spiral line round the spire. The inner walls of the whorls are either fused together so tightly that they form a spool-shaped plug or columella, or they are separated by a space of varying width forming a hollow cone down the middle of the shell known as the umbilicus, which often has an opening in the centre of the under side of the shell (the umbilicus). In species with a wide, open umbilicus (e. g. *Helicella itala*), the spiral of the whorls can also be seen from the under side. The last whorl, forming the aperture, is generally larger than the rest (body whorl), the remaining whorls forming the spire, which often projects above the body whorl.

The direction in which the whorls are coiled is also an important character. The majority of shells are coiled to the right (dextral) and only in the family Clausiliidae and a few species of the genera *Vertigo* and *Jaminia* are they normally coiled to the left (sinistral). We can tell whether a shell is dextral or sinistral by holding it with the aperture facing us and the apex uppermost. If the mouth or aperture is on the

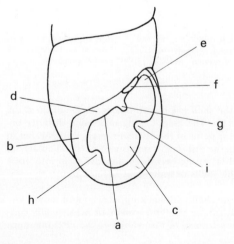

Fig. 4. Main features of the aperture of a shell (*Chondrula tridens*).
a — parietal wall, b — columellar part of aperture, c — palatal wall, d — parietal callus, e — upper corner of aperture. Teeth: f — angular lamella, g — parietal lamella, h — subcolumellar lamella, i — palatal lamella (fold).

right side the shell is dextral; in the reverse case it is sinistral. Very occasionally a dextral species will produce a sinistral example and *vice versa*.

The columella is not always straight, but is varyingly coiled in a spiral round the ideal axis of the shell. The coiling is sometimes so extreme that the turns of the columella allow us an axial view of the shell from the bottom right to the top; such shells are described as strophostylic (e. g. in the genus *Eucobresia*). Shells with a poorly developed columella, which blocks the view, are known as orthostylic (the majority of gastropods). Shells with a clearly distinguishable umbilicus are always orthostylic. The umbilicus varies from being very narrow and perforate (e. g. *Trichia unidentata*) to wide and shallow (e. g. *Discus rotundatus*). In adult specimens with a narrow umbilicus, the latter may be closed from below by the widened columellar edge or a reflected lip of the aperture margin. In part of the under side, with the umbilicus in the centre, there is sometimes a dimple or a funnel-shaped depression, which is known as the umbilical region or field.

During the life of the gastropod the whorls of the shell grow steadily wider — either evenly, when the width of each new whorl is in a given proportion to the one that went before and the shell grows regularly (as in the genus *Discus*), or unevenly, when the shell grows irregularly. In addition, we distinguish whorls that enlarge quickly (loosely coiled, as in *Helix pomatia*) and whorls that enlarge slowly (tightly coiled, as in *Discus rotundatus*). The degree of convexity is another important character. Whorls with an almost circular cross section are described as very highly convex or tumid. The whorls of most shells fit tightly together, so that the shape of the cross section is influenced by the convexity of the walls of the preceding whorls and varies from widely semicircular to narrow and sickle-shaped. Sometimes a keel or ridge is formed round the periphery of the shell; the keel may be simple (in the freshwater genus *Anisus*), or it may take the form of a beaded ridge (in the freshwater genus *Planorbis*). In a number of species the circumference is marked by a rounded crest (e. g. *Discus rotundatus*), which is sometimes indistinct (e. g. *Trichia*

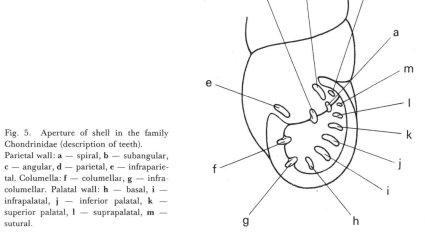

Fig. 5. Aperture of shell in the family Chondrinidae (description of teeth). Parietal wall: **a** — spiral, **b** — subangular, **c** — angular, **d** — parietal, **e** — infraparietal. Columella: **f** — columellar, **g** — infracolumellar. Palatal wall: **h** — basal, **i** — infrapalatal, **j** — inferior palatal, **k** — superior palatal, **l** — suprapalatal, **m** — sutural.

unidentata). Some species have a sharp keel only when they are young; with advancing age the keel grows steadily blunter, until, at the aperture, it completely disappears (*Aegopis verticillus*). The presence of a keel is often indicative of a juvenile specimen. The suture can be shallow or deeply incised. In flat keeled shells the suture generally runs directly along the keel or just below it, giving the shell a lenticular appearance (e. g. *Helicigona lapicida*).

The shape of the aperture corresponds roughly to the cross section of the last or body whorl and it has three walls. The wall of the penultimate whorl at the aperture is termed the parietal wall, the part adjoining the columella the columellar wall and the outer free wall of the last whorl the palatal wall. As a whole, the aperture is generally elliptical or oval, but its contours are usually interrupted in the parietal part, giving it a truncated appearance. The aperture can also be round, semicircular, trilobate or auriculate. The place where the parietal and the palatal wall meet is known as the upper corner.

The edge of the mouth — the margin — is modified in a number of ways. If the wall of the last whorl has a sharp edge, with no folds or thickening, the margin is described as simple (in the family Zonitidae). Sometimes, however, the margin is widened and the edge is folded outward to varying extents (e. g. in the genus *Helicigona*). If the edge curves outward and is then tucked in again, we have an infolded margin (e. g. in the genus *Granaria*). Very often the margin is reinforced by a curious thickening known as a lip. An inturned and thickened margin — and generally the presence of a lip as well — indicates that the shell has stopped growing and that the gastropod is now adult. Most species have a margin only on the columellar and the palatal wall, while on the parietal wall it is interrupted; this is known as a discontinuous margin. On the parietal wall there is a thin layer of shell secretion contrasting with the rest of the outer surface of the shell, from which it differs as regards its colouring, lustre and (particularly) its surface texture. This is the parietal callus and sometimes it is raised like a door-sill, joining the two edges of the margin across the parietal wall, in which case we speak of a continuous margin.

In some families, genera or species, the area of the aperture is made smaller by projecting tooth-like or lamellate structures which are known as teeth and very often they stretch deep inside the shell (in the genus *Orcula*), while in other species

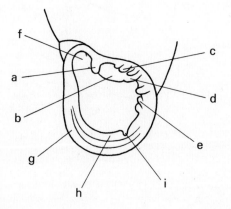

Fig. 6.   Aperture of shell in species of the family Clausiliidae.

a — superior lamella, b — inferior lamella, c — interlamellar folds, d — processes of inferior lamella on margin, e — folds on columellar part of margin, f — sinulus, g — lip, h — palatal callus, i — basal groove.

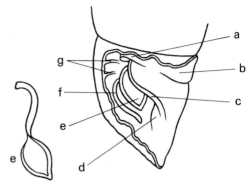

Fig. 7. View inside aperture in the family Clausiliidae (the palatal part has been removed).
a — spiral lamella, **b** — superior lamella, c — inferior lamella, **d** — subcolumellar lamella, **e** — clausilium (closure plate), **f** — lunule (semilunar fold), **g** — palatal folds.

they may be confined to small bosses situated along the margin or further inside the aperture (e. g. in the genus *Pupilla*). Some species have very complicated 'dentition' (e. g. Clausiliidae, Pupillidae, Chondrinidae). In addition to true teeth we find in the aperture a different type of teeth — primarily structures on the palatal segment of the margin which arise from the lip (in some species of the family Helicidae). Yet another feature of the aperture is a basal groove in the floor of the aperture, leading perpendicularly to the margin (in the family Clausiliidae); on the outer surface, behind the margin, it forms a crest on the neck. In addition to the lip, there may be a further thickening, deeper inside the aperture, of varying shapes, colours and sizes; it is termed the palatal callus and sometimes it unites with the lip. On the outer surface of the shell, just behind the margin, there is sometimes a longish thickening or nuchal callus, which is often differently coloured from the rest of the shell. In aquatic prosobranchial gastropods (e. g. in the genus *Fagotia*), the margin is interrupted by a deep notch — the siphonal sinus — at the division between the columellar and the palatal wall: this structure houses the siphon, an extension of the mantle.

The surface sculpture of the shell is a very important character in the identification of gastropods and should be examined with a lens or microscope. It is comparatively rare for the surface to be completely smooth (as in the genus *Cochlicopa*) and as a rule it is grooved, either transversely or axially (perpendicular to the suture) or longitudinally or spirally (parallel to the suture). Axial lines are more common than spiral ones. If the individual grooves or ribs are of roughly equal thickness and occur at regular intervals, the grooving is regular (e. g. *Granaria frumentum*); if they are of unequal thickness and their distribution on the surface is irregular, we speak of irregular grooving. Grooving can be very faint, barely distinguishable or pronounced. Raised areas between the grooves produce faint ribbing (in the genus *Granaria*), but the shell can also be (strongly) ribbed, if striking furrows and ridges appear on it (e. g. *Helicopsis striata*). In longitudinal or spiral grooving the grooves are mainly very fine, so that they give rise to spiral lines. If the spiral and axial grooves are almost the same thickness and density, they produce a regular reticulate pattern (in the genus *Aegopis*). In ribbed shells, spiral grooving is generally manifested in the form of cross folds in the furrows between the individual ribs. If the shell is very finely grooved, axially and spirally, the result

13

is a microscopic reticulate structure which can be seen only with the aid of a magnifying lens (e. g. the genus *Aegopinella*). Other shells have large numbers of square or rectangular impressions like indentations on their surface, separated by raised and more or less regular parts forming a rough latticework which reinforces the wall of the shell. The surface can also be granular and composed of large numbers of densely distributed tubercles (*Helicigona lapicida*). Some shells (e. g. *Acanthinula aculeata*) have pronounced spines. These structures already originate in the inorganic calcareous layer. Conchiolin (the periostracum or outer shell layer) participates in the formation of some structures, but in old shells which have lost their surface layer they disappear. Some shells are hairy, the hairs being long and usually curved extensions of the periostracum. The hairs can be permanent, remaining for the life of the snail, or deciduous, being formed in the juvenile shell only. When lost, as in subfossil shells, they generally leave dimple-like scars (e. g. *Trichia hispida*) which are visible when using a microscope.

The thickness of the shell wall is another important character. We differentiate between very thin-walled, flexible shells containing little calcium (in the family Vitrinidae), thin-walled shells (in the family Zonitidae), thick-walled shells (e. g. in the genera *Zebrina* and *Helix*) and very thick-walled, massive shells (in the genus *Lithoglyphus*). Some shells are fragile and easily broken (in the family Zonitidae), others are strong (in the genus *Helicella*). Although the strength of a shell is usually directly proportional to the thickness of its walls, there are some very strong shells with thin walls (in the genus *Chondrina*). The walls of the shells are sometimes damaged by corrosion, especially in the case of gastropods living in an acid environment with the apical parts of the shell the most affected.

The lustre of the shell is another important character. We distinguish shells with a high gloss, those with a moderate lustre (the majority) and matt (lustreless) shells. Lustre is usually in inverse proportion to the degree of grooving, glossy shells having a smooth surface.

The colouring of a shell is generally associated with the calcareous layers, particularly the prismatic middle layer. Brown shades predominate among most European molluscs, but occasionally we find whitish, milky, yellow, orange and red shades. Variegated colouring is relatively common, consisting of spots, blotches, zig-zags, spiral bands and less often axial bands. Sometimes various parts of the shell — the margin, the lip, the parietal callus etc — are coloured differently from the rest. The transparency of the walls of the shell is likewise largely associated with its colouring as well as its thickness. Some shells are colourless, with completely transparent walls, like glass, often with a greenish tinge (e. g. in the family Vitrinidae) with the colour of the body showing through in the live specimen. We differentiate between highly transparent to almost transparent, weakly translucent and opaque shells.

The general shape of a shell is determined by its ratio of height to width. On this basis, shells are classified as flat (wider than they are high), high (taller than they are wide) and spherical (both dimensions are roughly the same). In the case of tall shells we distinguish tapering, conical, cylindrical, fusiform and ovoid forms. Very often two types are combined (e. g. ovoid-cylindrical — *Pupilla muscorum*). Shells whose height and width are almost the same are roughly spherical (e. g. in the genus *Helix*), but their spire is generally conical, so that we describe them as spherical with a conical spire (e. g. *Arianta arbustorum*). In some aquatic species belonging to the genus *Lymnaea*, the shell is much dominated by the body whorl and the large aperture, so that it is described as auricularly enlarged. Among flat shells are sub-globular forms with a relatively conical spire (*Monachoides incarnata*) and forms with a wide umbilicus and a squatly conical or mildly bulging spire, which we describe as compressed-rounded (in the genus *Helicella*). Strikingly flat shells with a very wide umbilicus are described as discoid; their spire is either level with the rest of the shell or lies in a shallow or funnel-shaped depression.

In almost every species abnormally shaped or freak shells are encountered, which are difficult to identify without considerable experience. Furthermore, among a quantity of normally coiled shells, from time to time we come across an odd example coiled in the opposite direction. For instance, we may find a sinistral shell belonging to a Roman snail (normally dextral), or a dextral shell of the normally sinistral species *Laciniaria biplicata*. Another abnormality occurs when the whorls are joined insufficiently closely together so that they appear to be more convex and more developed than they are normally. Such cases are known as scalariform shells, a character which can be inherited genetically. Quite often we find shells which are only partly scalariform, in which the whorls are at first normal and become malformed only from a given point: sometimes abnormalities occur when growth resumes after hibernation. The most bizarre of these malformations are to be seen in the members of the freshwater family Planorbidae, whose normally discoid shells sometimes turn into towering structures bearing no resemblance whatsoever to the original form. Further random anomalies are caused by injury, which can produce the most diverse morphological deformities. 'Decollation' is an unusual type of deformity which occurs when the upper end of the visceral hump shifts to the lower whorls, so that the apical part of the shell collapses and snaps off. This is a regular phenomenon in the species *Rumina decollata*, which plugs the open end of the shell, and it is also occasionally to be seen in species of the family Clausiliidae.

In some gastropod families, the shell is reduced to varying extents. The greatest reduction is to be found in the slug genus *Arion*, when a vestige of the shell remains only in the form of chalky granules below the skin of the mantle shield. In the members of the family Limacidae, a residue of the shell has been preserved as an elliptical or oval 'slug' plate concealed by the mantle. Progressive reduction of the shell can be seen in the family Vitrinidae. Whereas *Vitrina pellucida* has a relatively large shell, into which the animal can withdraw completely, the genus *Semilimax* has very flat shells, strikingly small compared with the animal's body.

In addition to reduction of the size of the shell, some gastropods have fewer whorls. This is most striking in the species of the family Ancylidae, whose shell is cap- or boat-shaped and only the tip of the apex shows any signs of coiling. In the genus *Theodoxus* (family Neritidae), the whorls have been reduced internally. Both the whorls and the suture have been preserved on the outer surface, but the structure of the inner walls is progressively lost and the shell dominated by the body whorl.

One of the characteristic features of the prosobranch gastropods is the operculum, which is permanently attached to the animal's body on the back of the foot and acts as a tight 'trap-door' when the animal withdraws into its shell. The operculum, part of the living structure which grows, should not, however, be confused with the epiphragm — a temporary structure of solidified slime formed by pulmonate gastropods to plug the mouth of the shell in times of drought or hibernation. The epiphragm may be thick and calcareous (as in the genus *Helix*), or like parchment (in the genus *Helicodonta*), but most often (in *Monacha cantiana*) it is just a fine, transparent membrane formed in the aperture.

The body

The body of snails consists of a bilaterally symmetrical foot and head and a coiled, asymmetrical visceral hump that fits into the spire of the shell (see Fig. 8). The foot, extruded from the shell, is used for locomotion. It is composed of strong muscles and is connected anteriorly with the head, which has a mouth and sensory organs. The ventral surface of the foot is known as the sole. Locomotion usually takes the form of regular, continuous gliding. If we place the snail on a transparent surface like the walls of an aquarium and observe it from below, we can see on the sole dark transverse waves of muscular contraction travelling at regular intervals towards the head. In pulmonates the waves of contraction are transverse, but in prosobranches they are longitudinal, passing from side to side as in *Pomatias elegans*. The sole slides over a thin layer of mucus secreted by a gland situated in the anterior part of the foot. The 'swimming' of aquatic gastropods is likewise actually crawling over a layer or raft of mucus on the under side of the surface film of the water. The thin skin on the back and sides of the body also contains large numbers of mucous glands. Mucus released into the network of furrows between the tubercles spreads over the whole of the animal's body, so that even in land gastropods the evaporation of water from the skin is reduced.

The head is not distinctly separate from the dorsal part of the body, but the sole is divided off by a furrow marked in some slugs by a foot fringe. The head of freshwater gastropods carries one pair of non-retractile tentacles, while the black eye spots are seated on eminences at their base. Land gastropods have two pairs of retractile tentacles. The eyes are seated on the thickened ends of the upper pair; the lower pair are shorter and eyeless. In prosobranch gastropods, the oral or mouth region projects forwards and downwards, like a small proboscis. In pulmonates the mouth is partly covered from above by a pair of adoral lobes or lips.

The mantle is a skin-fold or pocket whose edge and outer surface secrete the shell. The mantle remains permanently inside the shell and its shape conforms to

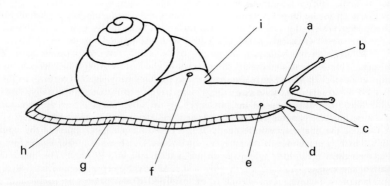

Fig. 8.   External morphology of a pulmonate land snail.
a — head, **b** — eyespot, **c** —tentacles, **d** — mouth, **e** — genital pore, **f** — respiratory pore (pneumostome), **g** — border of foot, **h** — sole, **i** — edge of mantle (collar).

Fig. 9. Detail of a radula of *Phenacolimax albopalliatus*.

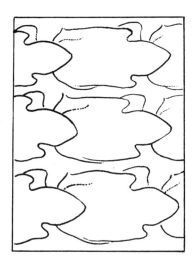

the shell's internal structure. Anteriorly and laterally it forms a mantle cavity with mainly respiratory function. The mantle cavity also contains the heart (usually composed of one ventricle and one auricle) and the single kidney alongside. In prosobranch gastropods the mantle cavity is open at the front and on its roof, on the left, is a pectinate or plumate gill. In pulmonate gastropods the mantle cavity forms a lung (its roof is covered with a capillary network of blood vessels) and is not open at the front except at the pneumostome or breathing pore, which can be open and closed by sphincter muscles. The same organization is to be found in aquatic gastropods which breathe air at the surface (e. g. *Lymnaea stagnalis*); many of them, however, have a secondary gill, in the form of various mantle appendages in the vicinity of the pneumostome (as in *Physa* species) or in the mantle cavity itself. The appendages may either be a temporary substitute for pulmonary breathing (in the family Planorbidae), or they may replace the lung completely (in the family Ancylidae or river limpets). Some gastropods (e. g. species of the family Lymnaeidae) fill their mantle cavity with water and are able to extract oxygen from the water. In prosobranch gastropods which left the water to live on land (the genera *Acicula* and *Pomatias*), the gill has been lost and the mantle cavity transformed into a lung.

The digestive system begins on the head with the mouth, continues with the oesophagus, crop, stomach and intestine, which is folded in loops, and terminates in the anus, at front of the mantle cavity. The mouth, which can be closed by lips, opens into the oral cavity, which in turn leads to the oesophagus and a large crop. The anterior part of the intestine is termed the stomach; opening into its posterior end is a combined gland — the hepatopancreas or digestive gland. On the roof of the alimentary tube of the mouth parts or buccal mass is a chitinous jaw for gripping particles of food, working in conjunction with the radula. The shape of the jaw, in the various groups of gastropods, is used in identification of species (see Fig. 10). On the under side of the oesophagus is a protruding structure known as the radula or tongue, the convex surface of which is covered with a fine chitin membrane and a quantity of minute teeth arranged in transverse and longitudinal rows.

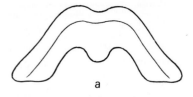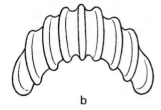

Fig. 10. Different types of gastropod jaws.
a — *Limax maximus*, **b** — *Cepaea nemoralis*.

This characteristic gastropod tongue, or radula, rubs the food against the jaw like a rasp or grater. Although the anterior end of the radula is constantly being worn down, and old teeth broken off and discarded, its posterior end never stops growing, providing a continual supply of new teeth. The general pattern of the radula, the number of teeth in the rows, the number of rows and the shape of the teeth are very varied and are likewise characteristic of given genera or species. As such the radula is important in identifying molluscs.

Gastropods have an open blood system with blood spaces instead of veins. The respiratory pigment is colourless, although a few have haemoglobin. Their usual blood pigment — haemocyanin — contains copper, which binds small amounts of oxygen and the bulk of the oxygen is dissolved directly in the blood. The heart, enclosed in a thin pericardium, consists of a single thick-walled ventricle and a single thin-walled auricle (atrium). The blood takes up oxygen from the capillary network of the lung and then transports it, via the pulmonary vein, to the auricle and from there to the ventricle. The ventricle expels the oxygenated blood into the arteries and after it has also passed through the arterioles it bathes the tissues, which obtain oxygen and food from it and discharge their waste products: the blood returns to the lung by a series of blood spaces rather than veins.

The nervous system consists of a nerve ring with pairs of ganglia which circles the oesophagus. Peripheral nerves springing from this central system lead to the sensory organs (the eyes and the organs of taste, smell and equilibrium) and to the body wall.

The most powerful muscles are those of the foot, particularly in the region of the sole, where they are used for locomotion. Another powerful muscle, attaching the gastropod's body to the internal spiral of the shell, is the columellar muscle, which is inserted on the middle of the columella and sends branches to the head and tentacle sheaths which retract the tentacles. By contracting the columellar muscle the gastropod withdraws into the shell.

Details of the genital organs are important in the classification and identification of molluscs. Among gastropods are both hermaphrodites (with male and female systems together) and species with separate sexes. All the prosobranch gastropods mentioned in this publication (apart from the hermaphroditic family Valvatidae) have separate sexes. These have relatively simple reproductive organs; the males have a gonad, a vas deferens and a copulatory organ (penis); the females a gonad, an oviduct and a vagina. Pulmonate gastropods are hermaphrodite and their repro-

18

Fig. 11. Reproductive system of *Helicella itala*.
a — gonad (ovotestis), **b** —small hermaphroditic
duct, **c** — albumen gland, **d** — spermoviduct or
large hermaphrodite duct, **e** — oviduct, **f** — vas deferens, **g** — flagellum, **h** — epiphallus, **i** — penis,
j — common genital pore (atrium), **k** — vagina,
l — dart sac (bursa telae), **m** — mucous glands
(glandulae mucosae), **n** — duct of spermatheca,
o — spermatheca.

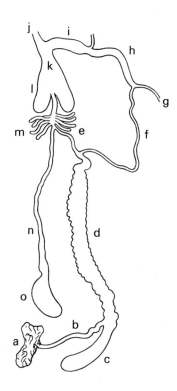

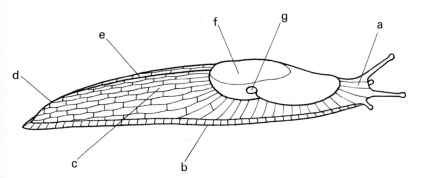

Fig. 12. External morphology of a slug.
a — head, **b** — sole, **c** — dermal tubercles, **d** — tail, **e** — dorsal keel, **f** — mantle shield, **g** — breathing
pore or pneumostome.

ductive apparatus is much more complex (see Fig. 11). The gonad is an ovotestis, producing both sperm and eggs. The duct of the gonad is in most cases divided, with one channel for transport of the sperm and the other for the eggs. Furthermore, pulmonates have accessory albumin and mucous glands and, in the oviduct of some families, a special evagination or dart sac. A thin, sharp-pointed chalky structure known as a love dart is formed in this sac and during mating the partners thrust it into each other as stimulation just before exchanging their sperm. In some snails (e. g. *Monacha cantiana*) darts are not formed and the dart-sac modified to an egersidium. The common genital aperture is on the side of the body, behind the head; in dextral species it is on the right, in sinistral species on the left. Although hermaphrodite gastropods can function simultaneously as both male and female, the sperms are formed earlier than the eggs. During copulation they lie with their right or their left side touching (according to the position of the genital aperture in dextral or sinistral animals). Each individual thrusts out its vagina, penis and dart sac from the genital pore and makes contact with the corresponding organs of the other animal. The sperm passes along the vagina of the recipient until it reaches an appendage far up the reproductive system known as the receptaculum seminis, where it is stored until the eggs are fertilized. After fertilization, albumen and egg-shells are deposited during passage along the large hermaphrodite duct.

Slugs, which have been modified by reduction of the shell (families Arionidae and Limacidae), have a different body structure (See Fig. 12). They do not possess a visceral hump, but their body consists practically entirely of the foot, which contains all the viscera on top. Their mantle usually takes the form of a fold of skin covering the dorsal surface at the front of their body like an oval or elliptical shield. It differs from the rest of the body and provides various features used in identification, like the position of the breathing pore and the surface pattern. Lying below the mantle may be remains of a shell, either in the form of a coherent slug plate (in the family Limacidae), or as chalky granules (in the family Arionidae). The dorsal part of the body between the edge of the mantle and the head is called the neck, while the part from the mantle to the tail end is the back. This is either rounded in profile (in the family Arionidae) or sharply keeled (in the family Limacidae) The lateral parts of the body are the sides and may have a foot fringe at the junction with the sole. The colour of the back and foot sole is important in the identification of slugs, but shows variation in some species, like the big *Arion*.

Morphology of bivalves

The shell

The bivalve shell consists of two valves which join at the hinge on the dorsal margin; they are also supported by a horny ligament. The nucleus of the valve or umbo, also on the dorsal surface, represents the embryonic shell, like the apex of a gastropod. The symmetry of the shell is important in the identification of bivalves. In most European freshwater bivalves the two valves are identical mirror images (equivalve). The symmetry of each valve is determined by drawing a line down from the umbo to the ventral margin — in symmetrical examples, e. g. *Sphaerium corneum* this line bisects the shell into two equal halves, since the umbo is cen-

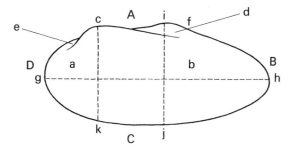

Fig. 13.   Main characters of a bivalve shell.
a — anterior part, b — posterior part, c — umbo, d — escutcheon, e — lunule, f — posterior slope, g—h — length, i—j — height, c—k — perpendicular connecting umbos, A — upper or dorsal edge, B — posterior edge, C — lower or ventral edge, D — anterior edge.

tral in its position. In *Unio*, where the umbone is distinctly to one side, a line drawn down vertically from it to the ventral margin divides the shell into two unequal parts: such a valve is asymmetrical (see Fig. 13). Muscle scars are also used in identification and these are shown in Fig. 15. The other parts of the shell are illustrated in Fig. 14 and 15. The dimensions of the shell, i. e. length and width are shown in Fig. 13.

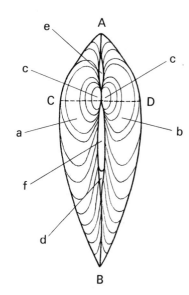

Fig. 14.   Valves of bivalve shell seen from above.
a — left valve, b — right valve, c — umbones, d — escutcheon, e — lunule, f — external ligament, A—B — length of shell, C—D — thickness of shell.

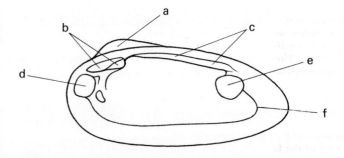

Fig. 15.   Hinge of bivalve shell (genus *Unio*).
a — umbo, **b** — main (cardinal) teeth, **c** — lateral teeth, **d** — anterior adductor muscle scar, **e** — posterior adductor muscle scar, **f** — pallial line.

One of the most important identification features of bivalve shells is the hinge, with its variable arrangement of teeth that are frequently characteristic of whole groups. In some genera the hinge is toothed, e. g. in *Anodonta, Dreissena* and *Pisidium*; in others it is not. The teeth radiating out immediately below the umbo are known as cardinal teeth and those alongside as lateral teeth. The shell valves can have thick walls deeply lined with nacre or mother-of-pearl (in the family Unionidae), or they may be thin-walled (most other freshwater bivalves).

Shells of freshwater bivalves have a very simple surface sculpture with mostly concentric grooving parallel to the outer margin. Ridges (umbonal lamellae), or small tubercles, blunt crests and folds are formed on the umbones of certain species. The embryonic (larval) valves are sometimes very distinctly divided off from the rest of the shell to form striking umbonal caps (in the species *Sphaerium lacustre*).

Bivalve shells are less brightly coloured than gastropod shells. Small species with thin walls are mainly translucent whitish, creamy or light greyish brown in colour; otherwise the shells are greyish brown to dark brown. Large species are predominantly dark brown to brownish yellow, often with a greenish tinge, as in *Anodonta anatina*, the duck mussel.

The body

As well as symmetrical valves, bivalves have also a symmetrical body. The dorsal part of the mantle is joined to the body, while its loose, leaf-like lobes line the inner surface of the valves, being attached by a muscle at the pallial line. Glands and fine muscles along the edges of the mantle give it a thickened ventral border. In some bivalves (in the families Sphaeriidae and Dreissenidae), the edges of the mantle are fused together, leaving only one free opening at the front for the foot and two openings for feeding and breathing — produced to tubes known as siphons — at the back. The siphons and foot can be seen in live specimens which extend in a dish of water.

The middle and dorsal part of the body form the trunk, from which rises the foot. The muscular foot is either wedge-shaped, with compressed sides (in the family Unionidae), or long and linguiform (in the family Sphaeriidae), and is used for burrowing and moving about. The respiratory organs — the gills — are paired lobes (outer and inner), symmetrical and lobular, and lie in the mantle cavity parallel with the mantle skirt.

The most important muscles are the two adductors (anterior and posterior), passing from one valve to the other, and their contraction closes the shell. In empty shells a scar is left where the adductor muscle fibres penetrated the inner surface of the shell in attachment (see Fig. 15).

In front, at the base of the foot, is a mouth, which has neither jaws nor radula. Food (microscopic organisms and organic matter) is filtered out by the gills and then proceeds by ciliary tracts along the gills to the mouth. The stomach of many bivalves contains a crystalline body (style) producing a secretory substance involved in digesting food. The digestive system continues with the intestine, which finally, as the rectum, curves into the dorsal part of the trunk and opens via the anus into an upper chamber in the posterior part of the mantle cavity. The heart has a single ventricle and two symmetrical auricles (atria); below it lie paired kidneys known as the organ of Bojan.

Bivalves have a similar nervous system to gastropods with nerves and ganglia, but much simpler due to their less active mode of life. Important among the sensory organs are the statocysts, the organs of equilibrium or balance. Freshwater bivalves have neither eyes nor tentacles.

In contrast to gastropods, bivalves have very simple reproductive organs. Fertilization usually takes place externally, in the water. In the families Dreissenidae, Unionidae and Margaritiferidae the sexes are separate; Sphaeriidae are hermaphrodite. The fertilized egg of *Dreissena polymorpha* develops directly in the water and gives rise to a free-swimming larva like that of marine bivalves. In time, the larva settles in a suitable spot, attaches by byssus thread and turns into a sessile adult bivalve. The fertilized eggs of members of the families Margaritiferidae and Unionidae are retained and develop in vast numbers, in the gill lamellae, into special larval stages termed glochidia (see Fig. 16). The glochidia are eventually released

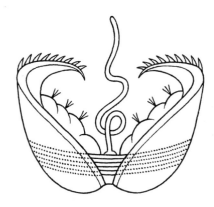

Fig. 16. Larva (glochidium) of a freshwater mussel.

into the water, where they live parasitically on fish until they are transformed to small bivalves and drop to the bottom to develop as free-living adult mussels. In the family Sphaeriidae the eggs develop inside the lobular gill without passing through a larval stage, so that the bivalve gives birth to live young resembling their parents.

Biology and ecology

Biology and ecology of land gastropods

Life cycle

Slugs and snails lay their eggs on the ground, in soil, in crevices, in rotting wood, or in damp spots under felled timber, leaf litter or under stones. The eggs are usually round and their number varies — in large species generally from 20 to 50, although there may be over 100. Most European non-marine gastropods have very soft, transparent eggs, while those of other species (e. g. *Discus rotundatus*) have a hard, opaque, chalky shell. The rate of their development depends chiefly on the temperature, but in most species the young are hatched within three to six weeks.

The eggs are laid mostly in the summer and autumn. Many slugs and some snails of dry habitats lay eggs in late autumn, when there is less danger of their drying up. The newly hatched young are miniature replicas of the adults; they develop directly without a larval stage. Most species attain maturity in one year, but the larger species take 2—4 years. When a snail stops growing, a margin or a lip is often formed on the aperture of its shell and sometimes a rib inside the mouth: it is then an adult. In some species, however, these features are missing (e. g. in the family Zonitidae and in slugs without a functional external shell); in that case, size, mating and internal anatomy give evidence of maturity.

Mortality among gastropods is highest in the initial stages of their life. The eggs — which are not guarded by the parents — may dry up or be eaten by other animals. The young are likewise liable to be killed by adverse weather conditions or by natural enemies, with the result that barely 5 % of the original eggs survive to maturity. In small species, the majority die during their first year, before they are able to reproduce, and comparatively few live on into a second season; in large species, about half the population dies every year. In contrast, a few individuals may survive 8—10 years or even longer.

Birds and parasites are responsible for a large proportion of losses. Among birds, the biggest culprits are thrushes, which often eat the larger gastropods (e. g. *Helix aspersa* and *Cepaea*). Their technique consists in picking up the shell by its aperture and smashing it on a stone. As a rule, one bird always employs the same stone, which in time becomes surrounded by a heap of broken shells. The bird may swallow some shell and remains of this can be found in the faeces of the bird. Slugs are less popular with birds than snails, because of the large amount of sticky slime secreted by their body. Apart from birds, snails are also eaten by shrews, hedgehogs and various rodents; shells bitten in two can be found in the passages of mouse burrows, or in a pile under timber.

Vertebrates are not the only enemies of gastropods, which are also eaten by other carnivorous gastropod species (e. g. *Aegopis verticillus*) and by predacious insects like glow-worms, rove beetles and parasitic flies.

Habits and food

As drought represents the greatest danger for most gastropods, they are therefore active at night or in damp weather. Most gastropods hide during the daytime in shady and cool places, under timber and stones, in leaf litter, amongst vegetation or a little way underground. Species living on the surface of stones or rocks are marvellously camouflaged, sometimes by their colouring and sometimes by a coating of microscopic algae and inorganic particles. In open, sunny habitats, however, the surface of the soil is often so hot that the land snails climb up plants and fence posts where it is cooler. Snails of hot dry places generally have a thick-walled, white shell which reflects solar radiation (e. g. the xerophilous species of the genus *Helicella*) reducing the amount of heat absorbed by the snail.

The best protection against drying up is for the snail to retire into its shell, leaving only the part of the mantle in the aperture unprotected. Once inside the shell the snail can seal the mouth of the shell against a rock surface or form an extra, temporary epiphragm and resist desiccation in this way. Large species usually survive long, dry summers in a dormant state (aestivation, i. e. 'summer sleep'). A thick epiphragm may also be produced by snails which hibernate over winter (e. g. *Helix pomatia*).

Although they have no shell, slugs have other ways of evading desiccation. They can move faster and they can bury themselves deep in the soil, for their slim bodies can gain access to small cracks in rocks or the trunks of a tree for protection. The outer layer of slime also helps to prevent them from drying up.

Most gastropods feed on rotting vegetation, fungi, algae and lichens; green plants (chiefly the fruit, seeds and the parts underground) are less often attacked. Gastropods bred under laboratory conditions can be fed on all kinds of substitute foods, such as lettuce, carrots, porridge oats and even moistened paper, since they are able to digest cellulose.

Some slugs belonging to the families Arionidae, Limacidae and Agriolimacidae very readily take to attacking crops and become pests which are exceedingly difficult to get rid of. Some gastropods live on carrion, but only a few are actually carnivorous; the only ones which devour other molluscs and their eggs are the members of the families Zonitidae and Vitrinidae, while the slug family Testacellidae eat earthworms. Most gastropods prefer a mixed diet and are opportunists: such flexibility contributes to their success as land animals.

Habitats

The majority of land gastropods do best on chalky soil, whereas few are to be found on very acid soil, such as moors and peat-bogs, where there is not enough calcium in the soil for the adequate construction of a shell. The shells of snails from acid localities are often very thin and fragile, requiring less calcium. Another important factor seems to be the physical state of the ground, with moist but loose soil attractive for egg-laying. Larger numbers of species and individuals are to be found in limestone regions: some species (calcicoles) are restricted to calcareous soils, but even snails which also live elsewhere are generally more abundant on limestone or chalk.

Climate is another important factor influencing the life of gastropods and in particular the local microclimate of the soil. On the whole, gastropods seem to prefer a warmer climate (the number of species increases towards the south of Europe), although in unprotected habitats high temperatures can be disadvantageous, because of the risk of heat stress and drying up. Most land molluscs like long periods of warm, damp weather, although there are some which have become adapted to hot, dry weather by modifying the structure of their shell, by their behaviour in learning to climb plants and seek shelter or by aestivating during drought.

The number of species in individual localities is also largely influenced by the diversity of the micro-habitat, e. g. the range of fallen leaves and branches, rocks, human rubbish, felled timber and the presence of trees and herbaceous plants.

Lastly, the mollusc fauna is influenced by man and domestic animals. While some molluscs have had their habitats destroyed by human impact on the land, others are able to adapt and thrive in gardens and waste places and their distribution may even be increased by man. Many of the more widespread species inhabiting different parts of Europe live in completely different habitats; at the periphery of their distribution area the majority are far more dependent on a given type of habitat and on the calcium content of the soil than in the centre of their area where they are less demanding, so that the description given of some habitats in the later part of the book must be regarded as only a general guide. Nevertheless, we can still define a few broad categories of habitats in which certain assemblages of molluscs are to be found.

Molluscs are richly represented in wooded regions, particularly on calcareous soil. Forests are the original, natural vegetation covering Europe and they provide gastropods with a damp and relatively uniform climate and an abundance of food and shelter. In central European forests with rubbly soil, the original woodland vegetation and sufficient calcium in the soil we can find about 50 species of molluscs. Tree-felling and an acid subsoil severely reduce the number of both species and individuals, so that we hardly find ten species in such surroundings. Some forest species live anywhere, in bushes, gardens, thickets and even on stony slopes, where they inhabit cold, damp crevices between the stones. By the sea or in the mountains, where the air is sufficiently humid, these forest species will actually live in the open. *Discus ruderatus, Ena montana, Faustina faustina,* most of the members of the family Clausiliidae and *Bielzia coerulans* are typical examples of forest snails.

Steppes — especially grazed grasslands on chalky ground — have a gastropod fauna that is capable of resisting drought and high temperatures, but over-grazing can seriously damage the balance of this fauna. Grassy dunes beside the sea have a similar open country fauna including, for instance, various species of the genus *Helicella, Pupilla muscorum* and *Cepaea* spp.

Swamps, marshes and fens are another clearly defined type of locality. Here the ground is always wet, so that the gastropods cannot burrow in it, but there is a wealth of vegetation providing shelter and a permanent high level of humidity. Marshes and the banks of rivers and ponds on a chalky substratum have a very characteristic fauna, only a few species of which live in any other type of habitat. Acid bogs, like dry ground, are very poor in molluscs and here we find only one or two species: one of them may be the calcifuge snail *Zonitoides excavatus.* In such habitats we may come across the empty shells of aquatic snails and bivalves and the shells of land snails mixed together. The members of the genera *Succinea, Oxyloma,*

Vetrigo and the species *Carychium minimum* and *Zonitoides nitidus* are typical inhabitants of acid wetland.

The fourth category of habitat includes rocks, cliffs and stony limestone slopes, which can likewise boast a number of characteristic rock rubble species. Some of them are forest species living on trees, but the rest live only on rocks in either shade or sunshine. The shell of many rock-dwelling species is longer than it is wide and these cylindrical and spindle-shaped snails live clinging to a rock or suspended from an overhang. This group, however, also includes large species with a rounded shell, which hide away in rock crevices when the weather is dry. Some of these snails have spread to the walls of ruins or houses and to recently disturbed ground of road cuttings, etc. (e. g. species of the genera *Alopia, Chondrina* and *Iberus*). Very small snails like *Vallonia costata* also live in the crevices of rock rubble.

High mountains — chiefly the Alps, also the Pyrenees and the Carpathians — have a number of local (endemic) species and subspecies which do not occur anywhere else. These have developed through isolation.

Secondary or man-made habitats, such as shrubberies, gardens, parks, roadsides and so on, often prove to be satisfactory habitats for some forest and open country species. It is in such places that we often find species spread by human influence.

Aquatic habitats — the last category — will be discussed in the next section.

Ecology of freshwater molluscs

Freshwater molluscs comprise a relatively small number of bivalves and prosobranchs and pulmonate gastropods. The bivalve and prosobranch species are most closely related to littoral marine forms. The basic prerequisite for their transition from salt to fresh water was adaptation of their body fluids to the lower concentration of the new environment (capacity for osmoregulation). Pulmonate gastropods, however, migrated to fresh water from the land; their type of respiration is still reminiscent of that of their terrestrial relatives using the mantle cavity as a lung and coming to the surface to breathe air.

Freshwater pulmonate gastropods are mainly bottom-dwelling (benthic) animals inhabiting the shallow water of lakes, fishponds, pools, rivers, streams, canals, marshes and ditches. It is rare for large populations to occur at depths of more than four metres. In some genera there are species which are to be found in a wide range of aquatic habitats across the world. Very large lakes and big rivers are inhabited by distinctly fewer gastropods than small lakes, fishponds and marshes, or small rivers, streams, canals and ditches. Gastropods living in stagnant water are generally associated with submerged or protruding vascular plants; those in flowing water live on stones and other hard surfaces like walls of bridges. Both the plants and the stones are at a depth where they receive sufficient light for plant growth and they are encrusted with microscopic plants and animals (diatoms, algae, bacteria, protozoans, fungi). The freshwater gastropods which live on this coating (they are predominantly herbivorous), have a specially adapted radula and digestive system. Only a few freshwater gastropods live on débris (rotting organic matter) in deep water in lakes or caves and only a few species are carnivorous. The species composition of an association of molluscs depends on the conditions of the micro-environment (food, the oxygen concentration) and the size of the habitat rather than its type (flowing or stagnant water). For example, the river limpet *Ancylus fluviatilis* is a typical inhabitant of small, fast-flowing streams, but it also occurs on the boulder-covered bed of lakes subjected to wave action, while the lake limpet *Acroloxus lacustris* is to be found on reeds and other hard material above mud with a low oxygen content, in slow-flowing rivers as well as in ponds.

The environmental requirements of most freshwater gastropods are very similar. In general, it can be claimed that more species are to be found in water with a high level of soluble calcium salts and abundant vegetation.

The concentration of soluble inorganic salts in fresh water is much more variable compared with sea water. For instance, the soluble calcium content can range from as much as 200-fold and the calcium:sodium ratio to over 50-fold. Freshwater gastropods occur in water with a calcium concentration of 2 mg/litre to 120 mg/litre or more. Of the 62 British freshwater molluscs, seven can live in extremely soft water (less than 3 mg Ca/litre) and 26 in relatively soft water (less than 10 mg Ca/litre, while six need at least 10 mg Ca/litre and two, which are strict calcicoles require at least 20 mg Ca/litre. *Ancylus fluviatilis* and *Lymnaea peregra* are examples of species which can live in water with poor plant production, since they feed on microorganisms in mud.

A further important factor influencing the occurrence of aquatic gastropods is the size of the habitat. As already mentioned, freshwater gastropods live mainly on the bottom, near the edge of shallow water. In some lakes, however, a few species form small populations at greater depths: the population of the pond snail (*Lymnaea* sp.) living in Lake Geneva at depths of 40—200 m is a classic example. Only the prosobranch species of the genera *Valvata* and *Bithynia* and the pulmonate species *Lymnaea peregra* and *Physa fontinalis* descend to any great depths in large lakes — *Lymnaea peregra* below 9 m and *Physa fontinalis* below 5 m.

Some species of the genera *Lymnaea, Physa* and *Planorbis* can live for a time at the surface, where they swim upside down under a thin film of water, gathering microscopic organisms with their ciliated sole.

The diversity of the molluscan fauna and the size of the various populations are likewise limited by the extremes of the environmental temperature. Species of the genera *Lymnaea* and *Physa* tolerate a temperature range of 0 to 44 °C.

Gastropods as intermediate hosts of parasites

Some freshwater snails (in particular members of the pond snail order Basommatophora) are intermediate hosts of parasitic flukes. The life cycle of the liver fluke (*Fasciola hepatica*), whose larvae develop in the snail *Lymnaea truncatula,* was known as long as 120 years ago. Since then, many biologists have studied the life cycles of various other parasitic flukes whose development is associated with molluscs. The two-suckered flukes of the order Digenea have a complicated cycle. For the eggs to be able to develop to the adult animal (parasitic in vertebrates), the fluke has to undergo complex transformation, during which it changes both its environment and its host several times. From the egg, deposited by the adult fluke and brought into the outside world, often by faeces of the vertebrate host, a small swimming miracidium larva will hatch. This is then attracted to water snails, whereupon it burrows into the snail host and starts to reproduce asexually. Eventually several hundred or thousands of free-swimming stages of the larval fluke (cercariae) will emerge from the snail. These may directly enter a third waiting (or paratenic host) by being eaten or they directly enter the final vertebrate host, either burrowing through the skin or by being eaten when encysted on a piece of plant or by eating the paratenic host. The infective larval fluke then matures to an adult in its final host.

Flukes belonging to the genus *Schistosoma*, which cause the disease known as schistosomiasis or bilharziasis, are a very serious medical problem. They are blood flukes and the resultant disease is manifested chiefly in the passing of blood in the urine or faeces, and is frequently fatal and certainly debilitating. The best known species, *Schistosoma haematobium*, causes 'Egyptian' (urinary) schistosomiasis. The intermediate host is *Bulinus truncatus*, a water snail belonging to the family Planorbidae. This particular form of the disease occurs chiefly in Egypt, but other forms are known in equatorial Africa, on the Atlantic coast of South America and in China, Japan and the Philippines. It also spread to the West Indies with the slave trade. The main sufferers are peasants working in artificially irrigated fields. Water snails abound in the irrigation canals, where they act as intermediate hosts for the larval stage of the fluke, which eventually emerge as free-swimming cercariae, bore their way into the skin of a human being and are carried by the blood stream to the intestinal and hepatic veins or bladder, where they settle down to mature. The eggs laid by the adult flukes penetrate the walls of the capillaries, are excreted in the human urine or faeces into the water channels and find their way back to the bodies of aquatic snails on hatching. Despite all attempts to control them by chemical and other means, the intermediate hosts of these flukes continue to spread further afield.

A few fluke families have also become adapted to land gastropods, through reduction of their free-swimming stages. For instance, *Urotocus tholonetensis*, which develops in the snail *Helicella arenosa*, has a completely terrestrial cycle. The snail eats the fluke's eggs and the early larvae (miracidia), which are hatched in the visceral hump of the snail, are transformed to sporocysts, which can remain where they are indefinitely. Not until the snail is eaten by a magpie are the flukes able to complete their development. In some terrestrial life cycles, infection of the definitive host is encouraged by a change in the behaviour and appearance of the intermediate host which makes it conspicuous. One example are the tentacles of amber snails (genus *Succinea*) infected by flukes belonging to the genus *Leucochloridium* or *Neoleucochloridium* which become red and enlarged and pulsate and are thus seen and eaten by birds, the final vertebrate host of the fluke.

We do not yet know the exact number of parasitic flukes which develop in gastropods, since many of the life cycles are still unknown. Among European species, the freshwater mollusc most interesting to parasitologists is the prosobranch snail *Bithynia tentaculata*, belonging to the family Bithyniidae, which acts as host to over 50 species of cercariae. The species of the freshwater pulmonate families Lymnaeidae and Planorbidae are also important. Almost 30 species of cercariae have been found in the Great Pond Snail (*Lymnaea stagnalis*), 20 in the Wandering Pond Snail (*Lymnaea peregra*) and 10 in the Great Ramshorn (*Planorbarius corneus*). Some of these flukes can cause swimmer's itch where large lakes are used for swimming by holiday makers.

Systematic classification of European families of non-marine molluscs

Phylum: *Mollusca*
Class: *Gastropoda*
Subclass: *Prosobranchia*
Order: *Archaeogastropoda*
  1. Family: *Neritidae*
Order: *Mesogastropoda*
  2. Family: *Cyclophoridae*
  3. Family: *Viviparidae*
  4. Family: *Valvatidae*
  5. Family: *Pomatiasidae*
  6. Family: *Hydrobiidae*
  7. Family: *Bithyniidae*
  8. Family: *Aciculidae*
  9. Family: *Thiaridae*
Subclass: *Pulmonata*
Order: *Basommatophora*
  10. Family: *Ellobiidae*
  11. Family: *Physidae*
  12. Family: *Lymnaeidae*
  13. Family: *Planorbidae*
  14. Family: *Ancylidae*
  15. Family: *Acroloxidae*
Order: *Stylommatophora*
  16. Family: *Cochlicopidae*
  17. Family: *Pyramidulidae*
  18. Family: *Vertiginidae*
  19. Family: *Orculidae*
  20. Family: *Chondrinidae*

21. Family: *Pupillidae*
22. Family: *Valloniidae*
23. Family: *Enidae*
24. Family: *Succineidae*
25. Family: *Endodontidae*
26. Family: *Arionidae*
27. Family: *Vitrinidae*
28. Family: *Zonitidae*
29. Family: *Milacidae*
30. Family: *Limacidae*
31. Family: *Agriolimacidae*
32. Family: *Boettgerillidae*
33. Family: *Euconulidae*
34. Family: *Ferussaciidae*
35. Family: *Subulinidae*
36. Family: *Clausiliidae*
37. Family: *Oleacinidae*
38. Family: *Testacellidae*
39. Family: *Bradybaenidae*
40. Family: *Sphincterochilidae*
41. Family: *Helicidae*

Class: *Bivalvia*
Order: *Eulamellibranchiata*
42. Family: *Margaritiferidae*
43. Family: *Unionidae*
44. Family: *Sphaeriidae*
45. Family: *Dreissenidae*

Zoogeography of European molluscs

Studies on fossil molluscs show that European land gastropods attained their present distribution during the Tertiary (Caenozoic) and Quaternary Eras. At the end of the Secondary (Mesozoic) Era, tropical genera predominated; they were either distributed circumtropically (i. e. round the equator), or were similar to genera inhabiting south-eastern Asia and Africa today.

With progressive cooling of the climate, the tropical fauna and flora began to retreat from Europe from the Miocene period (late Tertiary) onwards. The main changes in the mollusc fauna were due largely to the onset and alternation of glacial and interglacial periods during the Quaternary. During the interglacials, rich forest associations comprising species still common today in submontane forests developed. Warmth-loving species, which now live only in southern Europe, were also present in abundance. Some species started to invade central Europe from the south and south-east and also, on a smaller scale, from the coastal areas of the west, while a number of Pyrenean species migrated as far north as the British Isles. Conversely, the glacial periods were accompanied by a 60—75 % drop in the number of species in central Europe and the only ones to survive were those capable of living in an open terrain.

The present-day central European molluscan fauna was formed towards the end of the last glacial period, primarily as a result of natural changes and later through increasing interference by man. Some ten thousand years ago, as the climate became warmer and drier, more demanding forest species began to migrate to central Europe from localities further south, while during the past 7,000 years or so, man's influence has made itself increasingly evident. In the first place, man interfered with and cut down the native climax forests, giving rise to more open country. Many species of molluscs were able to adapt themselves to the new conditions and today they are found typically living in the vicinity of man (e. g. *Alinda biplicata, Discus rotundatus, Cepaea hortensis, Helix pomatia*). A number of new immigrants have become characteristic inhabitants of cultivated country, e. g. *Cepaea nemoralis, Oxychilus draparnaudi* and, as a new steppe-dweller, the arid country xerophilous species *Helicella obvia*.

Recent molluscan associations form a complicated mosaic in which natural habitats and associations ranging in type from substitute to explicitly anthrophilic (bound to the presence of man) alternate. The original fauna has in many regions been relegated to a few, limited areas and is thus of the nature of a relict.

In Europe we can distinguish roughly four main zoogeographical mollusc groups. The first consists of molluscs which occur on several continents and it is composed chiefly of holarctic species distributed in Europe, the north of Africa, Eurasia, north-eastern Asia and North America; it also includes palaearctic species (missing in North America), west palaearctic species (found in Europe, North Africa and western Asia), Eurosiberian species (inhabiting Europe and northern Asia, particularly Siberia) and European species, which are confined to Europe or may extend into Asia Minor, western Siberia and/or northern Africa.

The second group includes molluscs occurring over a wide area in one part of Europe. Central European species live chiefly in central Europe, but they are closely associated with molluscs whose range stretches further west, north or east and which are consequently known as central European-west European, central European-north European and central European-east European. Closely associated with west European species are Atlantic species living along the Atlantic coast of Spain, France and the British Isles, up the coast of Norway far to the north and along the coast of the North Sea and Baltic countries far to the east. Here there is a high rainfall and damp climate. Boreomontane species, which live in northern Europe and the mountainous regions and lowlands of central Europe, form a special group. Their area was broken up by climatic changes at the end of the Quaternary Era. In the cold phases or ice ages of the Pleistocene period (the early Quaternary), they inhabited most of the ice-free parts of central Europe, i. e. including the lowlands. In the Holocene period (the late Quaternary), when it grew warmer, they were progressively displaced further and further north and to higher altitudes in the mountains, where they still find suitable conditions. They are also still to be found in certain localities at lower altitudes, where they persist as isolated relicts.

The third group comprises species inhabiting southern Europe. Since southern Europe developed differently from the rest of the Continent (from a different tectonic plate), it has its own particular fauna forming a separate group. South European (meridional) species live mainly in the European countries bordering the Mediterranean and in the adjoining regions, Mediterranean species in a narrow zone stretching across the countries of the European Mediterranean and its islands and sometimes extending to Asia Minor or North Africa (circum-Mediterranean). Species which stretch from the Mediterranean along the Atlantic coast far to the north (e. g. to Great Britain) are described as Atlantic-Mediterranean. Species occurring in the steppes of eastern Europe — particularly the regions round the Black Sea (the Pontus Euxinus) are broadly described as pontic, although sometimes they extend to central Europe via the lowlands of the Danube. Species common to the Black Sea and Mediterranean regions are known as Pontic-Mediterranean. This group also includes species whose distribution can best be described as south European (Balkan) or Alpine-Mediterranean. One important feature of all these species is that in central Europe they form a substantial part of xerophilous and open country steppe associations and reach the northern limit of their distribution there. Some of them are relicts from bygone warmer ages, in particular the last of the interglacial periods (Riss-Würm).

The fourth category covers molluscs inhabiting a limited area in the great mountain ranges of Europe. They include Alpine (or east Alpine), Carpathian (or west Carpathian), Alpine-Carpathian, Carpathian-Balkan and Pyrenean species, etc. Ecologically they are mainly forest- or rock-dwelling species relatively closely associated with a mountainous terrain. The molluscs living in grasslands at the edge of mountains and in the intervening valleys are rewarding material for zoogeographical studies, because in the past their range was constantly changing, i. e. advancing and retreating. Some Alpine and Carpathian species penetrated mountainous regions in central Europe (e. g. the Bohemian massif), where their northern or western limits stopped, while other Alpine and east Carpathian species invaded the west Carpathians. These repeated changes of area resulted in numerous relict species and forms, a study of which provides valuable information on the palaeogeographical development of Europe in the most recent geological period.

Species of molluscs which have survived from preglacial times are known as preglacial relicts; those which have survived from the ice ages (chiefly on high mountain ranges or in northern Europe) are termed glacial relicts. Many of them occur today in only one, geographically restricted area; those are known as endemic species and their isolation is due to climatic and geographical factors which prevented them from spreading any further. Endemic species are also to be found in warm regions and lowlands cut off from similar places by high mountains; these are the remains of warmth-loving fauna from the interglacial periods and they are therefore known as interglacial relicts.

The influence of man on the molluscan fauna and its conservation

Apart from physical and chemical factors, man has also taken a hand in modelling the countryside for the past 7,000 years. He has changed the face of nature and has created new conditions — not only for cultivated plants and domestic animals, but also for a new flora and fauna, including molluscs. Man's interference with nature increases from year to year and in the course of the last hundred years there has been a significant change in its intensity and scale through mechanization and urban development.

Man has cut down most of the original forests and has drained swamps to acquire arable land and pasture, but these activities — felling, the removal of rotting wood, draining of the soil, grazing by domestic animals and regular ploughing — have all combined to make the ground unsuitable for many species of molluscs. In some cases, however, man has formed secondary habitats which have proved quite satisfactory for some species. In fact, the spread of artificial habitats like gardens, parks, greenhouses, roadside verges and railway embankments has led to a considerable increase in the distribution of many species. The expansion of open country has resulted, in some regions, in the partial or complete disappearance of forest-dwelling molluscs, while conversely, it has meant the formation of suitable habitats for those of open country, which in relatively recent times have spread northwards from the south — in many cases through the agency of man.

Although man's activity on the land dates back thousand of years, it was not until the technical revolution started that he turned his attention to water. The time involved has been relatively short, but the changes have already been far-reaching. In general, the effects have been generally harmful to molluscs, although there have been isolated cases of increased production of single species. Research initiated 50 or more years ago has demonstrated reduction of the number of species in the fauna of several lakes. Environmental changes, including pollution from eutrophication and acid rain, have reduced the number of pulmonate snails, while on the other hand explosive proliferation of the species *Bithynia tentaculata* and *Sphaerium corneum* has occurred. Loch Leven, famed for its salmon, has been studied thoroughly for over 80 years. For the whole of this time it has been continuously enriched with nutrients and during the past 30 years six species of snails have disappeared from it.

Dam-building likewise seldom makes a positive contribution to the number of freshwater gastropod species. The occasional elevation of the water level can sometimes create conditions for marginal populations (particularly large species), but when the water level sinks again the survivors are mostly only small pulmonate and prosobranch snails, which are not dependent on shallow marginal water to the same extent.

The effects of mild organic pollution of water by man (small amounts of sewage water and farmyard waste) are often indistinguishable from a natural increase in pollution (mostly seasonal or local overproduction of organic matter from plants and animals). The situation in European rivers is very critical, however. Their pollution by organic and inorganic waste (from industry sewerage and fertilizers) has reached such a degree as to turn them into 'sewers' from which molluscs have completely or at least partly disappeared. Some species and whole associations have died out and many others are likely to suffer the same fate. The best known example of the extinction of a species from many of its former localities, is the Pearl Mussel, but original steppe and forest species are also disappearing in the same way. That is why it is so necessary that every malacologist should ascertain and keep a record of localities of any natural habitats with a full complement of the original species of molluscs. Such places are very important for the reconstruction of bygone natural conditions in a given region and they therefore have every right to protection. Senseless devastation of certain localities should be prevented, such as the burning of grass on hill- or roadsides, or the felling of the last remnants of primary green-woods, for such places are today the last refuge of many native animals in our culti-vated countryside and by destroying them we make the fauna and our own environ-ment the poorer. Although they are very often inconspicuous species, their disap-pearance is a sign of impairment of biological balance whose consequences will be felt by future generations if not by ourselves.

It is becoming increasingly manifest that it is not sufficient to protect single spe-cies in small areas. The immediate vicinity of such nature reserves has been so much altered by human agencies that the reserves themselves are permanently af-fected by their surroundings. Large scale interference with the countryside, such as water management projects and aerial spraying have a particularly adverse effect on the flora and the fauna. In some regions they eventually lead to considerable cli-matic changes which naturally have a negative effect on the original structure of the flora and fauna. It is therefore essential to save whole regions, complete with whole biocenoses (ecosystems, comprising both plants and animals) of a large enough area to be ecologically viable and stable. Although many nature reserves and protected areas were intended for the preservation of rare plants or vertebrates, by conserv-ing habitats they likewise provide protection for whole associations of molluscs too.

The healthiest biological communities (biocenoses) are to be found today in mountainous regions with spreading forest complexes, whose unsuitability for agri-culture meant that they were long left intact. Nevertheless, even here felling and grazing have in time done damage to original habitats. Exposure of the soil has led, on steep slopes, to increased erosion and to landslides. In such regions, attempts are being made to limit the catastrophic effects of man's activities by creating na-tional parks and protected regions within which again there are special, strictly guarded reservations intended primarily for the protection of relict and endemic species.

The maintenance of mountain (montane) environments is not just the responsibi-lity of the authorities or the workers in national parks, however. It is up to all of us to see that nature is protected — in the mountains or wherever else we may happen to be.

Collection, preservation
and identification of molluscs

Collection

Before we actually begin collecting, we must first of all look out potentially productive sites, where the maximum number of species will be found. In general, limy and chalky ground are the most promising. If we are not properly acquainted with the region, it is best to consult a geological map to find out where limestone rocks outcrop. A few unsuccessful attempts are often made before finding the right localities. The best time for collecting gastropods is usually during damp weather at the end of the summer and autumn. Good results can be obtained when it is raining or after a storm. Since gastropods can measure anything from 2 to 200 mm, different methods have to be employed to find them. Large species from 5 mm upwards are relatively easy to see, although the majority are not active during the daytime and must be looked for under wood or stones, in natural litter or on the ground, tucked away under plants. For this type of search a small rake is useful. At the same time, we should take care not to damage the habitat and to put stones and pieces of wood back in their place as they were found. In about an hour we ought to have collected all the larger species. Collecting in the woods is often hampered by the poor light and small species are easily overlooked, while others are so small that we cannot find them easily in the field even in a good light. For these, the best method is to collect leaf litter and the surface layer of the soil in cotton or linen bags, in which the material does not turn mildewy if kept for a time as it would in polythene. Back home, in good light, we spread the contents out on paper and pick out the shells with a fine moistened paint brush or very fine flexible forceps. If we use our fingers we are liable to damage or destroy fragile shells. If the amount of material collected is very large, the work can be made easier by letting the litter dry and then sifting it through a sieve with meshes 3—4 mm in diameter. In this way the coarser material (including clearly visible larger shells) is left in the sieve and small shells can be picked out of the rest.

There are, however, special types of sieves which we can take with us for field work. The traditional sifter is a long fabric bag open at both ends, whose upper end is attached to a metal frame with a handle. Half way down the bag there is another metal ring with a handle, surrounding a wire sieve with approximately 10-mm meshes. The bottom of the sifter is tied together with string to catch the material which falls through the sieve. Litter and top-soil come into the top of the bag, which is thoroughly (but gently) shaken in all directions to sift the material through. If we are collecting samples from different spots, each time the material is transferred from the sifter to a fabric bag. On returning home, the samples are spread out on newspaper to dry and then passed through a sieve with approximately 0.8-mm meshes to get rid of dust and other tiny particles which would not contain the shells of adult snails. We then sift the remaining material through at least two sieves with different sized meshes. In this way several fractions are obtained from which it is much easier to choose our specimens than from the original, ungraded material. The best way to pick out the smallest species is under a binocular microscope.

Molluscs on damp fallen leaves, moss and dead grass in damp meadows can be shaken out manually on to a white sheet. The damp material is spread out on newspaper or a large tray and left to dry. It is then shaken until most of the tiny shells have fallen out, together with the dust. To remove the dust we sift the material with a fine sieve and can pick out the shells from the residue without any difficulty.

Sometimes a sweep net (commonly employed by entomologists) can be used for collecting as in the dog's mercury or grass of woods. The herbaceous vegetation is swept quickly and vigorously, and among the insects and other creatures which land in the net are also some molluscs. When collecting gastropods clinging to rocks or trees, a cotton, linen or plastic sheet is spread out below a rock or a tree and then, with a brush, we detach the gastropods so that they fall to the ground and on to the sheet.

When collecting aquatic species a fine-meshed net made of nylon or some other strong fabric, with a folding metal frame attached to the end of a stick is used. Growths of aquatic vegetation are worked with the net along with fragments of dead plants or stones with snails attached to them. Molluscs occurring in mud are collected by sifting the mud with a metal or plastic kitchen sieve, the small snails and bivalves (*Pisidium*) being picked out from the sieve. Molluscs living in springs and streams are similarly collected.

Very rich collections of dead shells can be obtained from alluvial material washed or dredged up on river or canal banks. Such material can be taken home or sifted on the spot, but we should not forget that for small species we often need a magnifying-glass or a stereomicroscope — the latter being better for the determination of individual species.

In collecting we should always remember the need for conservation and protection of the habitat. In the case of common species it is possible to build up a large series of specimens without endangering the species in the given locality, but with rare species collecting should be limited to empty shells and only a minimum number, if any, of live adult specimens taken. Destruction of the environment does even greater damage than reckless collecting and we should therefore do our best not to disturb the ground and vegetation. On collecting expeditions a notebook should be taken to enter detailed information on every locality visited. For collecting small species a small bottle or box is necessary, while large snails and slugs can be placed in fabric bags, in both cases together with damp plants, moss or moistened paper to prevent their being crushed. If plastic bags and lunch boxes are used, the animals should not be left in them very long. Snails can survive quite a long time in a dry cardboard box or a fabric bag, but slugs must be put into well-aired containers with moistened paper or leaf litter. Carnivorous species should be kept apart from other molluscs.

Each sample in the collection should have a label marked with a number (the same as the number in the notebook), or with full details on the locality, habitat, date, collector and eventually the identification. Since molluscs have a weakness for paper, especially if it is wet, the label should be stuck on the outside of the tube or bag. Another alternative is to place the label in a plastic bag and drop that into the container or to use plastic dymo tape for locality numbers, which will not be eaten.

Preservation and preparation of specimens

The great majority of molluscs can be identified from their shells and collections of shells are therefore the most common. Slugs must be preserved in denatured alcohol (about 70 %) but this causes the body to shrink and to lose its colour, so an exact description of the living animal's colouring should be written down and a close-up coloured photograph taken.

Empty shells can be kept in almost any type of container (small cardboard or plastic boxes, screw-top bottles, etc.) but instead of boxes and bottles of different shapes and sizes it is best to use standard glass tablet bottles (measuring 5—7 cm) arranged neatly in boxes or in drawers. For very small species transparent gelatin capsules, like those employed for certain drugs, can be used. Since sunshine — and any long exposure to light — eventually bleaches the colour from shells, when the collection is not in use it should be kept in the dark, in a drawer or a cupboard.

Live molluscs must first have the body removed as this soon begins to decay and to make an unpleasant smell. The animals are killed by drowning in dilute Epsom salts or by plunging them into boiling water and removing the body of large species with forceps or a bent pin. If some of the body snaps off and is left in the tip of the spire, the shell is left in a damp, sealed vessel until the flesh rots and comes away by itself. Small species are treated in the same way to avoid damaging them by the above operation. The shells are then rinsed clean by a fine jet of water directed into the aperture, or they are washed in a sieve to save the operculum in those species of prosobranchs which have one. It is virtually impossible to remove the body of the very smallest species and we therefore either leave them until they are absolutely dry, or pickle them a few days in alcohol and then dry them. When the shells are absolutely dry they are placed in air-tight containers, because otherwise the water in them starts to condense and the shells lose their colour. The best containers are screw-top bottles with a plug of cottonwool inside them. Sometimes shell collections are visited by a museum beetle or some similar house pest, whose larvae devour any remains of the bodies left inside the shells. As distinct from entomological collections in malacological collections they can be welcome helpers.

Every box or tablet bottle should contain only one species from only one locality and carry a label with full documentation, i. e. the name of the species, the site of the find (the locality), the habitat, the collection date and the name of the collector and/or of the person who identified the gastropod. Some collectors number the items of their collections and keep a written record in a separate catalogue. This is not a system that can be recommended, however. For instance, if the catalogue is lost then most of the scientific value of the collection is gone, for today our overstocked museums quite rightly refuse to accept material not accompanied by proper documentation. Such a loss is frequently irreplaceable, since Man is constantly changing the European countryside and a collection from a particular region may in time be the only evidence that such a fauna was once at home there.

Identification of molluscs

Our basic aids for the identification of most species are a good magnifying-glass (× 10) and a millimetre rule. For the smallest species, however, a stereoscopic binocular microscope and metal calipers are more accurate means of measurement.

Most species can be identified from the character of the shell, with the shape and size being the most important immediate criteria for the determination of the family. Fresh adult shells are much easier to identify than old and worn or immature shells, which often lack some of their diagnostic characters. In live specimens it is sometimes difficult to see the important characters round the aperture and the umbilicus and so the first thing to do is to clean out the shell.

Other diagnostic features (apart from shape and size) include the character of the larval whorl or protoconch, surface sculpture, the size of the whorls and the manner in which they expand. These are generally sufficient for identification of the shell and there are therefore only a few gastropods which need to be dissected. If we are not sure of our identification of a shell, it can be compared with specimens in a museum which have been correctly determined by a specialist. Such shells are a valuable part of comparative collections.

As distinct from snails, slugs do not possess usually an outer shell. Their main diagnostic characters are size, the presence or absence of a keel, the appearance of the slug plate, the position of the respiratory pore (pneumostome), and the surface texture of the mantle shield. Additional characters for identification include colour and striping, the size and shape of the tubercles, the colour and viscosity of the slime, colour of the foot sole and tentacles and presence of a foot fringe. As a rule, slugs do not always need to be dissected and this is only done when we have failed to identify our slug on the basis of all its external characters. Readers who are interested will find details on dissection techniques in the relevant specialist literature.

How to breed molluscs in aquaria and terraria

Like certain small vertebrates, molluscs can also be kept in aquaria and terraria. Freshwater species of ponds give the least trouble. Two or three small ram's-horns or pond snails can be kept in a one-litre glass jar; larger species require a two-litre jar or small aquarium. The water should be taken from the place where the animals were collected together with substrate (sand, mud) and plants such as Canadian pondweed and water milfoil. The aquarium is first of all set up with the plants and bottom mud and then left for a few days to establish; this also allows us to make sure that there are no leeches in the water since they suck the blood of water snails. Lastly, the molluscs are introduced into the aquarium, which is then kept in a place where it has plenty of light, but is not exposed to direct sun.

The keeping of slugs and snails in a terrarium is much more difficult, as there are several conditions which constantly need checking. The larger gastropods (the Roman snail, large slugs) each require two litres of space, moderately large species (e. g. the Banded snail and middle-sized slugs) one litre and small species (e. g. *Trichia, Perforatella* and *Helicella* species) a quarter of a litre, so that if we enlarge our living collection we must also enlarge the terrarium accordingly.

The type, as well as the size, of the terrarium must likewise be considered. Most gastropods need plenty of light, air and humidity and cannot be kept very long in glass jars. Small insectaria (small vivaria for keeping insects) made of varnished wood or metal are very practical. Except for the solid floor and one wide side made of glass, the walls are all made of very fine wire-netting. The floor should be perforated in a few places to let excess water run out; it is covered with a layer of coarse gravel to drain the water away. On top of the gravel there is a layer of loose soil and leaf litter mixed with fragments of limestone. The thickness of this layer is determined by the size of the gastropods. For large species it should be about 10 cm deep, to allow them to burrow and lay their eggs. Lastly, this layer is topped by moss, turf, rotting wood, fallen leaves and/or a few stones, according to the gastropods' ecological requirements. In at least one corner there should always be moss since it holds water well and helps to maintain humidity. Sometimes a small earthworm can be introduced, to keep the soil well aerated.

Other plants can also be added to the terrarium — e. g. ivy, daisies, loosestrife and others — and see which of them its inhabitants like the best. Those can be left in the terrarium as a permanent supply of food. We can also offer gastropods stinging-nettles, dandelions, spinach, beans, chopped raw potatoes, carrots, turnips, cucumber, marrow, bananas, tomatoes and sweet fruit, but only in small pieces so as not to litter the terrarium with decomposing remains. Cleanliness is absolutely essential and all food remains should be promptly removed and the terrarium kept clear of excess of excreta and slime. Moss should be changed every week and the entire contents of the terrarium should be cleaned every month and the old soil replaced by new; the whole terrarium should also frequently be sprayed with water.

In addition to species which like moisture, it is possible to keep gastropods which like warm and dry conditions, such as *Helicella* species and *Zebrina detrita*. In that case we should not water the terrarium so often and it does not need a drainage layer or a perforated floor. For a few hours every day it should go out in the sunshine to air.

British land and freshwater snails and slugs

In Britain there are about 88 species of land snails (including 2 prosobranchs), 26 slugs, 37 pond snails (9 species of prosobranchs and 28 pulmonates) and 28 freshwater bivalves, making a total of 179 species excluding brackish water examples and some garden introductions. (About half of these are illustrated in this book, either as colour photographs or as line drawings.)

The history of the British slug and snail fauna dates almost exclusively from the end of the last Ice Age. During the Pleistocene, a period of alternating ice ages and warm interglacials, the snail and slug fauna changed considerably with the climate and was almost completely exterminated in Britain during the last, more extensive glaciation. In the period following this, from 15 000 to 8300 BC, the glaciers receded and warmer climatic conditions returned. Britain was then attached to the Continent and various animals and plants migrated across the land bridge and began to colonise. It was some time before forests re-established, so the early molluscs colonising Britain were hardy species adapted to open country situations.

Between 10 000 and 8000 BC, there was a warmer period (known to geologists as the Allerod Oscillation) which provided opportunities for warmth-loving species to move into Britain. During the Post-glacial from 8300 BC, forests started to establish themselves, and steadily the open country landscape was almost completely replaced by pine and birch woodland in the north and mixed deciduous oak-wood in the south. Many of the earlier open country snail and slug colonists decreased in numbers with the loss of their habitat.

The warmer conditions led to a rise in sea levels as water, once locked up as ice, was returned to the ocean: the Irish Sea first separated Ireland and later the English Channel separated the rest of Britain from the Continent around 5000 BC. A number of warmth-loving snails had already migrated in from the Continent via the land bridge — species like *Acicula fusca*, *Azeca goodalli*, and *Pomatias elegans* (p. 52) — but the latter two, although they reached mainland Britain, never established themselves in Ireland as the Irish Sea had already formed by the time they arrived. At this time, the Boreal Period, the country was largely covered with climax forest which provided little habitat diversity and a predominantly woodland snail and slug fauna. Whilst at this time man was still a hunter-gatherer of the Mesolithic culture living in low population densities, there was little human impact on the forest.

With the development of farming in the Neolithic, about 3000 BC, clearings were made in the native woodland for grazing or arable land. The woodland molluscs then started to decline with reduction of their habitat and the cooling of the climate after the end of the Allerod Oscillation. Snails like *Acicula fusca*, *Ena montana* (p. 74), and *Helicodonta obvoluta* (p. 140) which were once widespread in Britain during the forest phase, have now been reduced.

In the early days of Neolithic agriculture, land clearance was on a comparatively small scale, there remained reservoir woodland snail and slug populations between the cleared areas and change was slow enough for species to adapt to new habitats. In Britain agricultural land developed gradually over nearly 5,000 years, contrasting sharply with the United States where the change happened in no more than 200 years. Thus many American species were unable to adapt to the new conditions, persisting only in the remaining old woodland and their place being taken on farmland by slugs and snails introduced on plants brought in by European settlers.

Cultivation of the land created a more diverse countryside with a mosaic of different habitats which were each colonised by characteristic snails and slugs. Ploughing provided looser soil which was appreciated by some species for burrowing and egg-laying. Walls, buildings and rubbishy areas provided new opportunities, and in southern England the Rock Snail, *Pyramidula rupestris* (p. 70), is found on old established walls, particularly those of castle ruins. The open country snails, which had been restricted by the almost total cover of the Boreal forests, started to expand their range again, and in the Iron Age species like *Abida secale* (p. 189), *Monacha cartusiana* (p. 130) and *Helicella itala* (p. 122) were more widespread in Britain than they are today. Tolerance of man's interference has resulted in the evolution of synanthropic or anthropophilic species which prefer to live near human settlements.

With time the snail fauna of Britain has (and always will) changed, reflecting the influence of climatic change and human interference, largely through modification of habitats. Whilst the greater part of our snail fauna had already arrived before Britain became a series of islands, various new species have subsequently been introduced. This is evident when we compare lists of shells from dated levels of archaeological sites with the modern fauna. In pre-Roman times the larger grassland snails were mainly *Helicella itala* and *Trichia hispida* (p. 136), other common grassland species of today, like *Monacha cantiana* (p. 197), *Candidula intersecta* (p. 196), *C. gigaxii* (p. 196) and *Cernuella virgata* (p. 128), came in later. A number of introductions are thought to have arrived with the Romans from Italy, who probably introduced them on plants and seed. Certainly *Helix aspersa* (p. 168), *H. pomatia* (p. 170) and *Monacha cantiana* (p. 197) are not known before Roman times and *Trichia striolata* (p. 136), originally a woodland snail, later became synanthropic.

Some introductions of snails like *Fruticicola fruticicola* and *Helicopsis striata* (p. 124) have not survived and are now deemed extinct in Britain. Other introductions like *Hygromia limbata*, *H. cinctella* and *Trochoidea elegans* (p. 124) have been known from flourishing colonies at limited sites for about a century but they do not appear to have spread. Several introductions have been associated with horticulture — Kew Gardens with plants from all over the world has many of these — and some are confined to greenhouses. Slugs in particular have travelled much around the world with garden plants. There are two slugs which have recently expanded their range. *Deroceras caruanae* (p. 195) was formerly known from a limited distribution on the west country coast, but in the mid 1960s it spread throughout Britain on cultivated land. More recently *Boettgerilla pallens* (p. 196), a rather worm-like slug, has turned up in a number of sites in Britain when it was previously only known from Eastern Europe.

Human interference in Britain's original landscape has resulted in a great change in the diversity and extent of all habitats. This has effected the numbers and distribution of our snail fauna as well as the rest of our wildlife. In recent years, the destruction of wetland and marsh has reduced the number of snails found on wet ground and since they are unable to adapt to drier conditions populations of wetland molluscs have become threatened with extinction. On the other hand the disturbance of the countryside and the creation in the past of a greater diversity of suitable habitats such as walls and hedgerows has, in some circumstances, actively helped snails and slugs.

Freshwater species have been less affected by man over the years and as a whole there is less variation in species of freshwater molluscs from country to country across Europe than for land molluscs. However, in the last century pollution of water from sewage, industrial waste and run-off of agricultural chemicals are having an effect on our waters and on the molluscs, in addition to the loss of habitat from the drainage of ditches and small ponds.

A considerable number of the molluscs occurring in the British Isles are widespread throughout Europe: these include: the two *Carychium* species, *Oxyloma elegans (= pfeifferi)*, *Succinea putris*, *Cochlicopa lubrica* agg., the three species of *Vallonia*, *Acanthinula aculeata*, *Pupilla muscorum*, *Ena obscura*, *Punctum pygmaeum*, *Discus rotundatus*, *Vitrina pellucida*, *Vitrea crystallina* agg., *Aegopinella pura*, *Nesovitrea hammonis*, *Oxychilus cellarius*, *Zonitoides nitidus*, *Limax maximus*, *L. cinereoniger*, *L. marginatus*, *Deroceras laeve*, *D. reticulatum*, *Euconulus fulvus* agg., *Cochlodina laminata*, *Trichia hispida* and the two species of *Cepaea*.

Another group of species consists of those which are often uncommon in Britain or of limited extent, being on the edge of their distribution range, but are more widespread on the Continent. Among these are *Pomatias elegans*, *Succinea oblonga*, *Truncatellina cylindrica*, *Vertigo moulinsiana*, *Abida secale*, *Ena montana*, *Phenacolimax major*, *Boettgerilla pallens*, *Monacha cartusiana*, *Hygromia limbata*, *H. cinctella*, *Helicodonta obvoluta* and *Helix pomatia*.

A third category flourishes particularly in the British Isles and is characteristic of the damp western oceanic climate. It includes *Acicula fusca*, *Azeca goodalli*, *Pyramidula rupestris*, *Lauria cylindracea*, *Leiostyla anglica*, *Spermodea lamellata*, *Oxychilus alliarius*, *O. helveticus*, *Zonitoides excavatus*, *Milax gagates*, *Macrogastra rolphii*, the three species of *Testacella*, *Cernuella virgata*, *Candidula intersecta*, *C. gigaxii*, *Monacha cantiana*, *M. (Ashfordia) granulata*, *Zenobiella subrufescens*, *Trichia striolata* and *Helix aspersa*. Of these, Britain forms an important part of the limited range of *Leio-*

styla anglica, Spermodea lamellata and *Oxychilus helveticus* while *Monacha (Ash-fordia) granulata* is an endemic species.

Molluscs of the western Atlantic coast of Europe are well represented in Britain while a few of the southern warmth-loving snails like *Pomatias elegans* (p. 52) are near the northern extent of their range in Britain and are therefore restricted to the southern half of the country. Species with an eastern European bias do not form part of the British fauna. A combination of high rainfall, a mild climate and limestone outcrops make parts of Ireland particularly rich in both numbers and species of land snails and slugs. The southern half of Britain also provides good collecting with its diversity of habitat and presence of warmth-loving species. Large parts of Scotland and Wales, although wet, lack the calcareous rock and have a less rich fauna of molluscs, although they yield special rare Arctic-Alpine relicts in the mountains.

Within the relatively small area of the British Isles, is a considerable climatic range, in temperature from north to south, in rainfall from west to east and with the additional influence of the Gulf Stream which has a warming effect on Cornwall, Devon and the south-west coast of Wales. The distribution of limestone also controls the range of some species, particularly those with thick shells.

Plates

Class: **Gastropoda**
Subclass: **Prosobranchia**
Order: **Archaeogastropoda**

Family: **Neritidae — Nerites**

Most members of this family are marine and only a few species live in fresh water. The shell as a whole is semi-ellipsoid or semi-ovoid, with very thick walls. The shell has $2^1/2$—3 whorls which expand rapidly and envelop each other so that the small spire protrudes only a little way above the surface of the dominant body whorl. The aperture is semicircular and the conspicuous white columella is flattened and shelf-like, the margin simple and sharp. The calcareous operculum attached to the back of the foot has the form of an incomplete single spiral. The three nerites illustrated differ in the pattern on the shell.

1. *Theodoxus danubialis* (C. PFEIFFER, 1828) — a Pontic-Balkan species. The shell has a short semi-ellipsoid form and the slightly prominent spire accounts for about one third of its length.
Colouring: the ground colour of the shell may be light greyish green, yellowish green or light orange brown, with large numbers of russet to dark reddish brown zigzag cross (axial) stripes.
Size of shell: length 9—13 mm, width 7—9 mm, height 4.5—7 mm.
Habitat: on stones in large rivers.
Distribution: from the Danube and its tributaries to the Black Sea, former Yugoslavia, northern Italy and the west of the European part of the former USSR.

2. *Theodoxus transversalis* (C. PFEIFFER, 1828) — an endemic species to the Danube. The spire accounts for one third of the length of the shell, which has $2^1/2$—$2^3/4$ whorls. Before reaching the aperture the suture dips sharply downwards, thereby giving the spire greater prominence.
Colouring: the ground colour of the shell is grey or yellowish grey, with three dark longitudinal or spiral bands; very occasionally the entire shell is black or yellowish brown without bands.
Size of shell: length 7—11 mm, width 5—7 mm, height 4—5 mm.
Habitat: gently flowing rivers.
Distribution: endemic to the middle reaches of the Danube and some of its tributaries.

3. *Theodoxus fluviatilis* (LINNAEUS, 1758), **Freshwater Nerite** — European. The shell, which has an elongate ovoid form, has an only slightly prominent spire which generally accounts for rather less than one quarter of its length. There are $2^1/2$ whorls and the suture distinctly dips before reaching the aperture.
Colouring: the ground colour of the shell is white or yellowish with variable brownish violet reticular markings which often merge to form three indistinctly circumscribed longitudinal or spiral bands; the pattern is extremely variable.
Size of shell: length 6—11 mm, width 4—8 mm, height 3—5 mm.
Habitat: stones in large, clean rivers and in large springs.
Distribution: the greater part of southern, western and north-eastern Europe, the Baltic region and the basin of rivers in the region of the Black Sea, where it forms several subspecies.

Order: **Mesogastropoda**

Family: **Cyclophoridae**
The members of this family occur in warm regions virtually world-wide. European species have a narrowly conical shell, usually marked with fine grooves. The rounded aperture can be closed by a deeply retractile operculum. The head has a short proboscis and the eyes are seated on slender protuberances at the base of the two tentacles. The European genus *Cochlostoma* comprises a large number of similar species of land operculates mainly inhabiting the Mediterranean region.

1. *Cochlostoma auritum* (ROSSMÄSSLER, 1837) — Dinarian. The fusiform shell is marked with alternating coarse and fine axial ribbing which terminates on the first third of the body whorl. It has $9-10^{1}/_{2}$ distinctly tumid whorls whose size increases regularly but slowly. The large, rounded aperture has an auricularly widened, flat, sharp margin with a distinct white lip.
Colouring: greyish white to yellowish brown, with a white margin.
Size of shell: height 8—15 mm, width 3.6—5.5 mm.
Habitat: prefers limestone rocks without any shade.
Distribution: forms several subspecies in the western part of the Balkan peninsula. Former Yugoslavia.

2. *Cochlostoma septemspirale* (RAZOUMOWSKY, 1789) — south European. The shell has $8^{1}/_{2}$ tumid whorls separated by a deep suture. It is marked with regular sharp axial ribbing (6—8 ribs to 1 mm). The aperture is usually rounded and the thick, white margin, which curls sharply outwards, consists of an inner and an outer part separated by a slight cleft. The small umbilicus is often obstructed by the widened columellar lip. The membranous operculum can be retracted deep inside the shell.
Colouring: greyish white to dull brownish red, with three rows of dark spiral spots.
Size of shell: height 7—8 mm, width 3.8 mm.
Habitat: rocks, rubbly slopes, rock faces, copses — always with a limestone base. Occurs in both exposed and shady habitats.
Distribution: a common species in the south and east of France and in Switzerland and Germany. Sporadic in Belgium.

Cochlostoma septemspirale laying eggs

Family: **Viviparidae — River Snails**

This family includes prosobranch gastropods with a short robust body, a short, wide foot and a head tapering off to a club-like snout. The tentacles are relatively long and shaped like a thick awl. In the males, the right tentacle is thicker than the left one and acts as an organ of copulation. The females retain the fertilized eggs and give birth to young. The shells of the young have rows of bristle-like spines.

The shell is much larger than the shell of other freshwater prosobranch snails and is easily identified from the three dark longitudinal stripes on the whorls. Male and female shells often differ in respect of their shape and size. The operculum — the characteristic structure of prosobranchial gastropods — has concentric growth marks.

This relatively small family is represented in fresh water on all the continents except South America. River snails — shut off from the outer world by their operculum — can survive for a time on dry land (e. g. if they are thrown up on the shores of large lakes by waves, or if their pool or ditch dries up). The snails live on fresh algae, on organic débris in the mud or on plankton, which is filtered off from the water during respiration. They tolerate both occasional pollution of the water and inclement climatic conditions.

Viviparus contectus (MILLET, 1813) (= *V. fasciatus*), **River Snail** — European. The shell is spherically conical, with a pointed apex, thin, transparent walls and very fine, irregular grooving. It has 6—6¹/₂ highly tumid whorls with a very deep suture between them. The aperture is almost vertical; it is irregularly and obliquely oval. The margin of the mouth is slightly blunted, but its columellar segment widens and thickens, so that it partly hides the narrow, but open umbilicus.

Colouring: the shell is brownish green and is generally marked with three brown, longitudinal or spiral bands, although sometimes they are absent.

Size of shell: length 30—50 mm, width 25—35 mm, height of aperture 16—20 mm.

Habitat: stagnant water at low altitudes, with abundant vegetation, including pools, creeks, fishponds and ditches. The snails live in the mud on the bottom and the greater part of their shell is therefore covered with slime and débris.

Distribution: a widely distributed species, especially in the lowlands of central Europe; absent in the most northerly and most southerly parts and in big mountain ranges. It stretches eastwards as far as the basin of the river Ob in Russia.

Family: **Viviparidae**

1. *Viviparus viviparus* (LINNAEUS, 1758), **River Snail** — European. The shell has an ovoidly conical form and thick walls much stronger than those of *V. contectus*. The apex is blunt and rounded. There are 5—6 mildly and almost regularly convex whorls. The obliquely pointed, oval aperture has a distinct, blunt upper corner and the outer edge slopes directly — and relatively abruptly — downwards from its insertion on the parietal wall. As distinct from the preceding species, the umbilicus of adult specimens is almost completely occluded by the columellar edge of the margin.
Colouring: the shell is a greyish yellow green to olive green, with three reddish brown stripes.
Size of shell: height 28—35 mm, width 22—25 mm, height of aperture 15—17 mm.
Habitat: between stones near the banks of large rivers and in canals and reservoirs communicating with a river.
Distribution: the basins of the larger European rivers, except in the most northerly and southerly parts, including the Balkans.

2. *Viviparus mamillatus* (KÜSTER, 1852) — Dinarian. This is very similar to the preceding species, but the shell is more swollen, with more convex whorls and a deep suture, and its lower part is more rounded. Compared with *V. contectus* it has less tumid whorls, a shallower suture, a blunter apex and a narrower umbilicus. The oval horny operculum has thickened edges and tapers off to a blunt tip.
Colouring: usually dingy olive yellow, but sometimes greyish olive green or olive brown, occasionally with faintly indicated reddish stripes.
Size of shell: height 35—40 mm, width 20—28 mm, height of aperture 17—22 mm.
Habitat: lakes and the rivers that feed them.
Distribution: Montenegro and Albania.

3. *Viviparus acerosus* (BOURGUIGNAT, 1862) — an endemic species. The shell has thick, strong walls and $5^{1}/_{2}$—$6^{1}/_{2}$ slightly tumid whorls. The apex is domed and rises to a noticeable point. The umbilicus is largely hidden by the columellar part of the margin. In addition, sexual dimorphism plays a marked role in the shape and size of the shell, male shells being more slender and having less convex walls than in *V. viviparus,* while female shells are more robust and have slightly more convex whorls.
Colouring: greyish yellow-green with three brown (and often only faintly indicated) stripes.
Size of shell: height 30—55 mm, width 23—38 mm, height of aperture 16—22 mm.
Habitat: stagnant or sluggish, muddy water in low-lying country.
Distribution: endemic to the Danube basin, from Vienna to the mouth of the Danube.

Family: **Valvatidae** — **Valve Snails**

The members of this family have a distinctly separate head and a partly retractile snout. The eyes are seated at the base of the long, thin and extremely retractile tentacles. A plumate gill emerges from the left side of the mantle cavity. The circular, spirally coiled operculum is a notable feature. This sole hermaphroditic family of the subclass Prosobranchia is represented in both flowing and stagnant water in the Palaearctic region.

Family: **Pomatiasidae**

This family is distributed over the warmer parts of the Old World. A characteristic feature of its members is the chalky operculum at the rear end of the body as well as the shape of the shell and mouth and marked spiral sculpture. The sexes are separate and the shells sometimes show slight signs of sexual dimorphism (the female shell is usually a little larger than the male shell).

1. *Pomatias elegans* (MÜLLER, 1774), **Round-mouthed Snail** — a Mediterranean and western European species. The shell is widely conical and thick-walled, with reticular ribbing, strong axial sculpture and $4^1/_2$—5 rounded whorls. The operculum is thick and chalky and when the animal withdraws into its shell it closes the aperture. The operculum bears spiral sculpture.
Colouring: the shell is greyish mauve to yellowish and is variably marked with dark spots or broken spiral stripes.
Size of shell: height 13—16 mm, width 9—11.5 mm.
Habitat: on limestone and chalk in open woods, copses, thickets, hillsides with chalky soil. The snail needs a friable soil for burrowing and is a strict calcicole.
Distribution: the Mediterranean countries and islands, Bulgaria, the Pyrenees, western Europe as far as Germany, the south of England and Wales; isolated localities in central Europe.

2. *Pomatias sulcatum* DRAPARNAUD, 1801 — west Mediterranean. The shell is ovoidly conical and rather dull, with pronounced spiral lines and thin, dense cross stripes. It has $5^1/_2$ tumid whorls, the last of which is somewhat flattened and distinctly widened at the umbilicus. The umbilicus itself is a small cleft only; the operculum can be retracted deep inside the aperture.
Colouring: very variable, brownish mauve, unicoloured, sometimes with a black stripe on the last whorl, yellow, reddish orange.
Size of shell: height 14—18 mm, width 9.5—12 mm.
Habitat: as for the preceding species (the two sometimes occur together).
Distribution: the south of Spain, the south coast of France, Italy, the west Mediterranean islands.

Valvata piscinalis (Müller, 1774)
(5 × 5 mm) Common Valve Snail

Family: **Hydrobiidae**

This family includes small to moderately large aquatic snails.

1. *Lithoglyphus naticoides* C. PFEIFFER, 1828 — Pontic. The shell is spherical, with a conical spire, and is almost opaque. It has $4^1/_2$ expanded but flat-sided whorls. The aperture is noticeably oblique and widely oval, with an obtuse-angled upper corner, and it accounts for over two thirds of the height of the shell. On the parietal and columellar segment the margin of the aperture curls inwards and forms a thick white lip which clings to the wall of the shell and completely closes the umbilicus. The operculum consists of a few rapidly widening whorls.
Colouring: varies from greyish yellow-green to greyish white.
Size of shell: height 7—12 mm, width 6.5—10 mm, height of aperture 5—7 mm.
Habitat: stones or mud near the banks of gently flowing rivers.
Distribution: originally in rivers flowing into the Black Sea. Has spread secondarily to the Baltic region and western Europe.

Family: **Bithyniidae**

2. *Bithynia tentaculata* (LINNAEUS, 1758), **Common Bithynia** — Palaearctic. The shell is ovoidly conical, with thin, transparent walls and very fine, irregular cross and longitudinal grooving. It has $5—5^1/_2$ mildly convex whorls and a relatively shallow suture, which gradually drops away before reaching the aperture. The aperture is a trifle slanting and is obliquely oval with a distinct blunt-angled corner at the top. The blunt margin is slightly widened and has a dark edge with a thin white lip, except on the parietal and columellar segment, where the edge curves inwards and the lip is thicker, so that it almost completely encloses the slit-like umbilicus. The operculum has concentric instead of spiral growth lines and is pointed at the top to match the shape of the aperture.
Colouring: very light brown; the shell is often covered with an opaque deposit.
Size of shell: height 9—15 mm, width 6—9 mm, height of aperture 5—6 mm.
Habitat: stagnant and flowing water at low altitudes — pools, reservoirs, canals, ditches. Commonest on stones near the banks of rivers and canals.
Distribution: the whole of Europe except the south of Greece and the north of Scandinavia.
Bithynia tentaculata is a frequent intermediate host of parasitic flukes.

Family: **Aciculidae**

This family is distributed over the western half of the Palaearctic region, where the snails frequent damp forest localities and live in litter and in the soil. They have a small (2—4 mm), glossy, cylindrical, blunt-tipped shell. The delicate horny operculum can be retracted deep inside the aperture. There are about 12 species.
Acicula fusca is the only species found in Britain.

Acicula polita Hartmann, 1840 (3 × 1.1 mm)

Family: **Thiaridae**

The members of this family are to be found mainly in subtropical and tropical regions. Some species are viviparous, others oviparous.

1. *Fagotia acicularis* (FÉRUSSAC, 1823) — Pontic. The shell is slender and conical, with a tall spine ending in a sharp-pointed apex and fairly thick, matt and slightly transparent shell walls. The 8—9 faintly convex whorls are separated by a shallow suture. The aperture is vertical, narrow and obliquely oval, with a sharply angular and tapering corner at the top; it also narrows at the bottom and below the bottom end of the truncated columella there is a shallow, rounded notch. The outer edge of the margin is straight; in fully adult specimens it is almost imperceptibly blunted, but otherwise it is sharp.
Colouring: variable; the shell is usually olive-tinged reddish brown to light greyish green, with a sharply defined yellow sutural stripe on the under side.
Size of shell: height 15—25 mm, width 5—8 mm, height of aperture 5.5—8 mm.
Habitat: lowland rivers, particularly on stones, submerged tree trunks and firm mud near the bank.
Distribution: rivers draining into the Black Sea, Hungary, Austria, former Yugoslavia and Asia Minor.

2. *Amphimelania holandri* (FÉRUSSAC, 1823) — south-east European. The shell is a swollen ovoid with thick walls. Its 5—7 convex whorls increase rapidly in size and the last one, which is more expanded then the rest, is smooth and carries thick longitudinal ribs or rows of bosses. The wide aperture is sharply pointed at the top and slightly drawn out and rounded at the bottom. The coiled operculum is formed of two rapidly widening turns.
Colouring: very light yellowish brown, plain or marked with 3—4 brown bands; sometimes completely black. The aperture is brown or pinkish inside.
Size of shell: height 16—22 mm, width 10—12 mm, height of aperture 9—12 mm.
Habitat: submerged stones in rivers and streams, particularly with fast currents.
Distribution: occurs in several forms in former Yugoslavia, Albania, Bulgaria, Austria and Hungary.

3. *Melanopsis praemorsa* (LINNAEUS, 1758) — Mediterranean. The shell has an elongate oval form, a relatively short but pointed spire and thick, smooth, glossy walls. It has five flat whorls and very shallow sutures; the body whorl is dominant and the whorls of the spire are almost always corroded. The aperture is pear-shaped, narrow at the top and rounded at the bottom, with a clearly discernible siphonal notch; the margin of the aperture is sharp-edged.
Colouring: cinnamon brown or black.
Size of shell: height 11—28 mm, width 6.5—12 mm, height of aperture 8—16 mm.
Habitat: mountain streams and small rivers, small fishponds, irrigation ditches, a high oxygen concentration is essential.
Distribution: occurs in a number of subspecies over practically the whole of the Mediterranean, Black Sea and Caspian regions.

Subclass: **Pulmonata** — **Pulmonates, Lung Snails**
Order: **Basommatophora** — **Aquatic Pulmonates or Pond Snails**

Family: **Physidae** — **Bladder Snails**

The members of this family have a narrow or bulging, ovoidly conical sinistral shell with glossy thin walls and no umbilicus. The family is represented on all the continents. Bladder snails are sinistral.

1. *Physa acuta* DRAPARNAUD, 1805 — Mediterranean. The shell is a pointed ovoid with a sharply conical spire and thin, but relatively strong walls. It is transparent and glossy, with fine reticular markings. There are 5—6 faintly convex whorls; the last or body whorl, which dominates the rest, is swollen and its sides are slightly compressed, narrowing at the base, with a trace of a ridge below the suture. The aperture is inversely auricular; it has a straight, sharp margin, which widens only in the columellar region, where it often forms a distinct, flat white lip. The parietal callus is very thin. The almost imperceptibly curved columella and the slightly convex parietal wall form an obtuse angle. The umbilicus is completely hidden.
Colouring: pale yellow-brown.
Size of shell: height 10—12 mm, width 6—7 mm, height of aperture = about two thirds of the height of the shell.
Habitat: stagnant and gently flowing water.
Distribution: the whole of the Mediterranean region, France, Belgium, Holland, the northern Caucasus and the basins of the rivers Dnepr and Don. It has also been brought by man to large parts of central Europe and other localities. A few populations occur in Britain, probably as introductions.

Physa fontinalis (LINNAEUS, 1758). See p. 188.

2. *Aplexa hypnorum* (LINNAEUS, 1758) — Holarctic. The fusiform sinistral shell has a slender, conical spire with a straight or slightly convex general outline and thin, but fairly strong, transparent, lustrous and indistinctly grooved walls. The six slender whorls increase regularly in size. The aperture is narrowly oval, with a sharp-pointed top, and is slightly hollowed out over a long segment of the parietal and collumellar part of the wall. The aperture has a straight, sharp-edged margin, which widens and thickens only along the columellar segment; the parietal callus is thin. The columellar and parietal segments form an only faintly curving line. The umbilicus is completely hidden.
Colouring: reddish brown to yellow.
Size of shell: height 12—15 mm, width 4.8—5.5 mm, height of aperture = approximately half the height of the shell.
Habitat: small stretches of stagnant water and grassy pools at low altitudes.
Distribution: most of Europe, northern Asia and North America.

1

2

Family: **Lymnaeidae** — **Pond Snails**

This family comprises large aquatic snails with a wide foot and a short head with triangular tentacles, which crawl along the under side of a thin film of slime which they form on the surface of the water and also on mud on the bottom. A special tubular outgrowth of the mantle allows their respiratory orifice to be protruded above the surface film to take in air. The great variability of the shell — due to the effect of different aquatic environments — led in the past to the description of a very large number of species. The family is distributed all over the world. The shells of *Lymnaea* are dextral.

1. *Lymnaea stagnalis* (LINNAEUS, 1758), **Great Pond Snail** — Holarctic. The shell is ovoid to elongate-ovoid with a tall, slender, sharply pointed spire with a clearly concave general outline. The walls of the shell are thin, fragile, partly transparent and somewhat shiny. Its surface is marked with fine and almost regular axial and spiral grooving, but these fine structures are often obliterated by coarse growth lines and by denting. There are $7 - 7^1/_2$ whorls which increase fairly quickly in size; the first ones are very small and the middle ones and last one are highly convex. The aperture is inversely auriculate; it spreads sideways and downwards and has a straight margin. The columella is strongly developed and in the upper part of the columellar segment it therefore forms a well developed columellar fold. The umbilicus is completely enclosed.
Colouring: light or dark yellowish brown; the shell is often covered with a coloured deposit.
Size of shell: height $45 - 60$ mm, width $20 - 30$ mm, height of aperture $23 - 35$ mm.
Habitat: stagnant or sluggish water with luxuriant vegetation at low altitudes.
Distribution: Europe, northern Asia, North America.

2. *Lymnaea auricularia* (LINNAEUS, 1758), **Eared Pond Snail** — Palaearctic. The shell is auricularly swollen and has a very small, sharply-pointed spire which usually projects above. It is thin-walled, fragile, lustrous and marked with fine irregular grooves. The first two of the $4 - 4^1/_2$ whorls are slightly convex and form the tapering tip of the spire; the others are more tumid and increase very quickly in size. The aperture is inversely auriculate; it has a simple, sharp margin, sometimes with an indistinct flat lip, and with an only mildly widened outer edge. The thin parietal callus overlaps the top of the columella and also covers the umbilical zone, so that the umbilicus is almost completely shut in. This species sometimes has to be dissected to distinguish it from similar forms of *L. peregra*.
Colouring: light yellowish brown.
Size of shell: height $25 - 31$ mm, width $25 - 30$ mm, height of aperture = a little less than the height of the shell.
Habitat: slow rivers, canals and large ponds in overgrown stagnant water at low altitudes.
Distribution: most of Europe, northern and eastern Asia; has been brought into North America.

Lymnaea truncatula (MÜLLER, 1774) See p. 188.

1

2

Family: **Lymnaeidae — Pond Snails**

1. *Lymnaea palustris* (MÜLLER, 1774), **Marsh Snail** — Holarctic. The shell is elongate-ovoid, with a sharp-pointed, conical spire, is fairly strong and opaque, with a dim lustre. The surface is marked with regular transversal and longitudinal grooving, but coarser growth lines are also frequent and denting is likewise common. The size of the six slightly and regularly convex whorls increases quite quickly, but the last one is not markedly swollen. The aperture is inversely auriculate, with a relatively sharp upper corner. The margin is straight and sharp and only occasionally widens a little at the bottom; the parietal callus is thin and flat but pale and distinct in adults.
Colouring: deep brown to dark greenish grey. The inner wall of the aperture (and the whole of the shell) is strikingly dark, ranging from dark violet brown to light chestnut. The colouring of the cross stripes is of very variable intensity, but it is always a deeper brown than in other members of the Lymnaeidae family.
Size of shell: height 20—35 mm, width 10—18 mm, height of aperture = roughly half the height of the shell.
Habitat: overgrown stagnant water at low altitudes, often at the edge of rivers or lakes and in marshes.
Distribution: A variable species with a series of ecological forms which are sometimes described as separate species. It inhabits Europe, northern Africa, northern Asia and North America.

2. *Lymnaea peregra* (MÜLLER, 1774), **Wandering** or **Common Pond Snail** — Palaearctic. The shell is ovoid, with a conical, pointed spire but subject to considerable variation. It is relatively thick-walled, but fragile, is slightly translucent, with a faint lustre, and is irregularly marked with fine grooves or ribbing. It has 4—5 mildly convex whorls whose size increases regularly and quickly; the last one expands irregularly, and this body whorl is dominant. The aperture is narrowly oval; it tapers towards the top, where it has a blunt upper corner. It has a simple, sharp margin, which widens only along the columellar segment. The parietal and the columellar segment together form a very faint arc or an indistinct, very obtuse angle. The narrow umbilicus is not hidden.
Colouring: light to dark yellowish brown; the shell is generally coated with a thick, variably coloured deposit.
Size of shell: height 11—22 mm, width 6—12 mm, height of aperture = about one third of the height of the shell.
Habitat: small stretches of water (brooks, springs, pools, bogs, ditches) at both low and high altitudes; sometimes it also occurs on dripping rocks and in periodic pools. In chalky water the shell is thick-walled, in acid and humic water it is thinwalled and frequently severely corroded. Because of its modest requirements and its powers of resistance, together with the Liver Fluke Snail (*Lymnaea truncatula*) it is often the only snail in poor mountain environments. In the Alps it occurs at altitudes of up to 2,800 m.
Distribution: Europe, northern Africa, inner and northern Asia. A very variable species which forms many subspecies and is adaptable to most freshwater habitats.

1

2

Family: **Planorbidae — Ramshorn Snails**

The main feature of the European species of this family is their flat discoid shell. Although it appears to be dextral (from its position during crawling and the organization of the aperture and the two sides), the morphology of the animal itself corresponds to that of sinistral gastropods (the respiratory and the genital orifice are on the left side). In flat, keeled forms the whorls often overlap. The head and the foot are relatively small and the tentacles are long and thread-like. Unlike other molluscs, the species of this family have red blood for storing oxygen.

The family is represented all over the world. Some are tolerant of temporary habitats which dry up and are able to close the aperture of their shell with a whitish, parchment-like epiphragm and survive for several weeks until the pool fills again.

Planorbarius corneus (LINNAEUS, 1758), **Great Ramshorn** or **Trumpet Shell** — Eurosiberian. The shell is thickly discoid, with the spire in a funnel-shaped depression and a mildly concave under side. Its walls are fairly thick, strong and faintly translucent, with a dim lustre; it is finely and irregularly grooved, with faint longitudinal or spiral lines which fade away on the last whorl, but are so pronounced on the initial whorls that the first three in the young snail are always distinctly reticulated. It has 5—5^1/$_2$ markedly rounded whorls, the last one of which is compressed from above and from below, especially in its last quarter. The aperture is widely kidney-shaped and slightly oblique and is made mildly concave by a dip in the parietal wall. The margin is simple and sharp-edged and widens somewhat at the top; a parietal callus is present as a mere trace.

Colouring: the ground colour is reddish brown to olive brown; the upper surface is often tinged blue or greenish grey and the under side white. The inner wall of the aperture is white just behind the margin and reddish brown further inside.

Size of shell: very variable, particularly as regards the main dimensions and their reciprocal ratio, the shape of the aperture and growth of the whorls. Height 10—14 mm, width 25—30 mm. Size may be affected by habitat.

Habitat: richly overgrown stagnant or sluggish water in lowlands.

Distribution: a substantial part of Europe, but not in the mountains and the most northerly and most southerly parts; also occurs in Asia Minor, in the northern foothills of the Caucasus and in Siberia as far as the basin of the river Lena.

Planorbarius corneus
Great Ramshorn or Trumpet Shell

Family: **Planorbidae — Ramshorn Snails**

1. *Planorbis planorbis* (LINNAEUS, 1758), **Ramshorn** — Palaearctic. The shell is discoid, with a mildly concave upper and under surface and relatively thick, strong, mildly translucent and faintly glossy walls marked with fine, regular grooving; the spiral grooving is somewhat less distinct, but the surface in general has a reticular structure. The upper surface of the 5—6 whorls is clearly convex, the under surface less so. The thread-like keel lies closer to the under surface of the shell. The last whorl is maximally twice the width of the penultimate whorl and the width of the spire accounts for over 45 % of the width of the shell. The oblique aperture has the form of a short transverse ellipse cut short in the region of the parietal wall; where the keel joins its edge, there is a clearly distinct corner. The margin is sharp-edged, simple or mildly blunted and its lower segment is in contact with the keel of the penultimate whorl.
Colouring: light brown.
Size of the shell: its size and the development of the keel have a tendency to vary.
Height: 3—3.5 mm, width 14—17 mm.
Habitat: overgrown stagnant water at low altitudes, muddy pools and creeks, ditches and swamps; also appears in periodic pools.
Distribution: most of Europe, northern Africa, Asia Minor as far as Syria, the region of the Caucasus and western and northern Asia to Lake Baikal.

2. *Anisus vortex* (LINNAEUS, 1758) **Whirlpool Ramshorn** — Eurosiberian. This snail has a small, thinly discoid shell with a mildly sunken spire and an almost flat under side. Unless covered with a deposit, the thin-walled shell is translucent, faintly glossy and covered with very fine, dense grooving. The upper surface of the 6—7 whorls is markedly, but not absolutely regularly convex, while their under side is almost flat. The simple, sharply prominent keel lies on the under side; the last whorl is almost treble the width of the penultimate whorl. *A. vortex* is more tightly coiled than the previous species. The very oblique aperture is irregularly transversely oval and is pointed on its external surface. The margin is simple and sharp and its lower segment is in contact with the keel of the penultimate whorl.
Colouring: pale brown.
Size of shell: relatively stable. Height 1—1.5 mm, width 8—10 mm.
Habitat: overgrown stagnant or sluggish water at low altitudes (pools, creeks, ditches, canals, fishponds); also lives in reeds on the banks of large rivers.
Distribution: most of Europe except the most northerly and most southerly parts: Siberia as far as the Yenisei.

Bathyomphalus contortus (LINNAEUS, 1758). See p. 188.

Gyraulus albus (MÜLLER, 1774). See p. 189.

Hippeutis complanatus (LINNAEUS, 1758). See p. 189.

Family: **Planorbidae — Ramshorn Snails**

1. *Helisoma trivolvis* (SAY, 1816) — Nearctic. The shell is moderately large, discoid and sinistral with five whorls; its surface is finely and axially ribbed. Much of the apex is pressed inwards to a hollow, but all the whorls are visible. The umbilical zone is deeply indrawn. The aperture is wide and ovally auriculate.
Colouring: yellowish brown to brown, with a reddish brown or purple stripe in the aperture.
Size of shell: height 10—15 mm, width 18—30 mm.
Habitat: in its native region in N. America the snail lives chiefly in lakes or in sluggish water with a muddy bed, among plants or on stones.
Distribution: forms several subspecies in Canada and the USA. Brought to Europe for the pools of botanical gardens and for aquaria.

Family: **Ancylidae — Freshwater Limpets**
The members of this family occur in the western part of the Palaearctic region. The cap-shaped, whorl-less shells are very different in appearance.

2. *Ancylus fluviatilis* MÜLLER, 1774, **River Limpet** — west Palaearctic. The cap-shaped shell is thin-walled and fragile. The blunt apex curves backwards and is twisted slightly to the right and is positioned near the posterior end.
Colouring: varies from reddish brown to light brown, yellow and greyish white.
Size of shell: length 4—9 mm. Width 3—7 mm, height 2—5 mm.
Habitat: it lives chiefly in flowing water, clinging to stones, and appears in considerable quantities in large springs, especially in karst formations.
Distribution: most of Europe, northern Africa, Transcaucasia.

Family: **Acroloxidae — Lake Limpets**
The shell is shallow and boat-shaped and its apex, which is more or less central, curves left and backwards. The limpets live on plants in clean stagnant water.

Family: **Ellobiidae**
The shell is fusiform and the widened aperture contains small teeth and folds. The snails live mainly in brackish water and along the coast, but a few species (e. g. the members of the genus *Carychium*) also occur in damp spots inland.

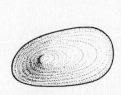

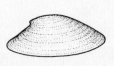

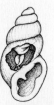

Acroloxus lacustris
(Linnaeus, 1758)
Lake Limpet (6 × 3.5 × 1.7 mm)

Carychium minimum Müller, 177
(1.8 × 0.9 mm) Herald Snail

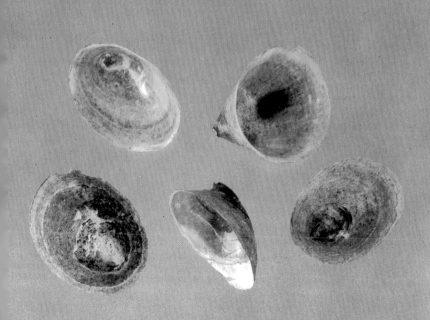

Subclass: **Pulmonata — Pulmonates, Lung Snails**

Order: **Stylommatophora — Land Pulmonates**

Family: **Pyramidulidae — Rock Snails**
This family comprises a few species inhabiting dry limestone rocks in the southern part of the Palaearctic region from Spain to Japan. One species only — *P. rupestris* occurs in Britain.

Family: **Vertiginidae — Whorl Snails** and **Chrysalis Snails**
These snails have a tiny (usually about 2 mm), oval or cylindrical shell, that is smooth or finely grooved and often has teeth in the aperture. They are distributed all over the world and live in the most diverse habitats, from the lowlands to high up in the mountains. *Truncatellina* species occur on dry, open, grassy and limestone substrates, whereas *Columella* and *Vertigo* species prefer marshy ground.

Vertigo pusilla (MÜLLER, 1774). See p. 190.

Family: **Orculidae**
The members of this family have a cylindrical shell larger (3—10 mm) than that in the Vertiginidae family. This small family is distributed throughout southern Europe and the Near East. The genus *Orcula* is represented by a few species in the eastern Alps.

Family: **Chondrinidae**
The species of this family inhabit warm regions, particularly in southern Europe, North America and south-eastern Asia. The majority live in open, dry localities and usually occur on limestone; some are specifically montane species.

Granaria frumentum (DRAPARNAUD, 1801) — Submediterranean. The shell has nine slightly convex whorls. The elliptical aperture is well provided with teeth. The margin is widened and incurved, with a white lip; the umbilicus is almost invisible. Colouring: light brown.
Size of shell: height 6.5—8 mm. width 2.7—3 mm.
Habitat: dry grassy hillsides and rocks in warm localities.
Distribution: southern Europe, southern and southeastern France, Switzerland, northern Italy, southern and central Germany, Austria, Hungary, the Czech and Slovak Republics and isolated localities in southeastern Poland.

Abida secale (DRAPARNAUD, 1801). See p. 189.

Pyramidula rupestris
(Draparnaud, 1801)
(1.7 × 2.7 mm)
Rock Snail

Vertigo substriata
(Jeffreys, 1833)
(1.7 × 1.1 mm)
Striated Whorl Snail

Orcula doliolum
(Bruguière, 1792)
(5.2 × 2.4 mm)

Family: **Chondrinidae**

Chondrina clienta (WESTERLUND, 1883) — Alpine-eastern Submediterranean.
The strong shell has a slender, conical ovoid form, it is slightly translucent, matt and with fine and somewhat regular axial lines; there are $7-7^{1}/_{2}$ whorls. The aperture is well supplied with teeth. The slightly widened margin has a thin, whitish lip. The umbilicus is very narrow.
Colouring: the shell is dark greyish brown or reddish brown.
Size of shell: height $5.5-7$ mm, width 2.5 mm.
Habitat: limestone rocks, from the lowlands to high up in the mountains.
Distribution: southern Sweden, southern Germany, Austria, isolated localities in the Czech and Slovak Republics, former USSR, Romania, Bulgaria, former Yugoslavia, Greece.

Family: **Cochlicopidae** — **Slippery Moss Snails**
The members of this family have an elongate-oval to fusiform shell. The margin is thickened, bluntly rounded and lipless. The family is distributed over North America and the western parts of the Palaearctic region.

Family: **Pupillidae** — **Moss Snails**
The shell may have teeth in the aperture and the margin is often thickened or incurved. This is a worldwide family. The commonest European species belong to the genera *Pupilla, Lauria* and *Argna.*

Lauria cylindracea (DA COSTA, 1778). See p. 190.
Leiostyla anglica (WOOD, 1828). see p. 190.

Family: **Valloniidae** — **Grass Snails**
European species belong to the subfamilies Valloninae (*Vallonia*, whose shell is $2-3$ mm wide) and Acanthinulinae (*Acanthinula, Spermodea, Planogyra* and *Zoogenetes*, whose shells are $2-4$ mm wide). Although *Vallonia* live in grass, *Acanthinula* and *Spermodea* usually occur in leaf litter of woods.

Vallonia costata (MÜLLER, 1774). See p. 191.

Vallonia pulchella
(Müller, 1774)
(2.5 × 1.3 mm)
Smooth Grass Snail

Cochlicopa lubrica
(Müller, 1774)
(6.2 × 2.6 mm)
Slippery Moss Snail

Pupilla muscorum
(Linnaeus, 1758)
(3.5 × 1.7 mm)
Moss Snail

Family: **Enidae**

The species of this family have moderately large (normally 8—20 mm), elongate, conical shells with slightly convex, regularly augmenting whorls. The edge of the aperture is widened and often thickened. The aperture may be supplied with teeth in the form of characteristic blunt bosses. This is a large family mainly inhabiting the Palaearctic region.

1. *Ena montana* (DRAPARNAUD, 1801), **Bulin** — central European. The shell is a tapering, blunt-tipped cone with thick, slightly translucent walls and only a faint gloss. It has 7—7¹/₂ mildly convex whorls of regularly increasing size. The elliptical aperture has an obliquely truncated parietal wall; it has a widened margin, especially alongside the columella, and a conspicuous lip. The very narrow umbilicus is hidden by the widened edge of the columella.
Colouring: the shell is brown, the margin pinkish white.
Size of shell: height 14—16 mm, width 6.0—6.5 mm.
Habitat: a forest species which forms small populations particularly in damp spots, overgrown with vegetation, beside the trunks of old trees or at the foot of rocks, in fallen leaves on the ground and among stones. Occurs in the Alps at altitudes of up to 2,600 m.
Distribution: The Pyrenees, the north-east of France, the south of England, Belgium, Germany, Switzerland, Austria, the Czech and Slovak Republics, Poland, Hungary, Romania, the Ukraine, Bulgaria, former Yugoslavia. Scattered occurrences in northern Europe.

Ena obscura (MÜLLER, 1774). see p. 191.

2. *Chondrula tridens* (MÜLLER, 1774) — Pontic-Submediterranean. The shell is cylindrically ovoid, strong, mildly translucent and faintly glossy, with 7—8 whorls. The aperture is elliptical, with large teeth on the parietal part, the columella and the palate. The margin is slightly widened and very blunt, with a thick lip which shows through the shell to the outer surface, just beside the margin. The umbilicus is incompletely closed.
Colouring: the shell is greyish or reddish brown and the lip is yellow (less often pink or reddish).
Size of shell: height 9—14 mm, width 3.8—4.5 mm.
Habitat: sunny, grassy, chalky hillsides in warm regions; a characteristic steppe species. Ascends to 2,200 m in the Alps.
Distribution: the European part of the Mediterranean as far as the Balearic Islands, France, Germany, Switzerland, the Black Sea countries, Austria, Hungary, the Czech Republic, Slovakia, Poland, the Caucasus, Iran. Scattered populations in the warmer parts of central Europe.

3. *Chondrula tridens albolimbata* (L. PFEIFFER, 1859) — south-east European. Compared with the preceding snail, this subspecies has a much more robust, coarsely built shell. The margin is lined with a thick lip; the teeth, although very pronounced, are relatively finely constructed.
Size of shell: height 13—16 mm, width 5—6 mm.
Habitat: the same as for *C. tridens*, but only at low altitudes.
Distribution: Bulgaria, Romania, Hungary; isolated localities in other parts of central Europe.

1

2

3

Family: Enidae

1. *Zebrina detrita* (MÜLLER, 1774) — Mediterranean. The elongate-ovoid, blunt-tipped shell has thick, strong walls and is mildly glossy and finely and irregularly grooved; on the upper whorls there are very fine longitudinal lines. The $6^1/2 - 7^1/2$ whorls increase regularly in size and are slightly convex. The aperture is narrowly elliptical, with a sharp angle at the top. The margin widens only along the columellar segment and on its inner surface it has a flat lip; it is extremely blunt. The parietal callus is very thin and finely granular. The slit-like umbilicus is hidden by the columellar margin.

Colouring: the ground colour is an opaque white, often with a yellowish or a pinkish grey tinge; the markings are transparent light or dark brown cross stripes, which sometimes undulate, break up into spots or disappear altogether.

Size of shell: height 17—27 mm, width 9—12 mm.

Habitat: dry, sunny spots, mainly on chalky soil (e. g. hillsides, steppes, vineyards); in the Alps up to 1,600 m.

Distribution: from the European part of the Mediterranean to Iran; France, Germany, Switzerland, Austria, the Czech and Slovak Republics, Hungary, Romania, Bulgaria, former Yugoslavia.

2. *Zebrina varnensis* (L. PFEIFFER, 1847) — an endemic species. The slender, cylindrical, thick-walled, glossy shell is irregularly grooved. In the middle the spire is cylindrical, but it tapers sharply upwards to a smooth, blunt apex. The size of the 9—10 somewhat convex whorls increases gradually; the last three are almost as wide as they are high and the very last one is slightly compressed at the bottom. The aperture is small, elongate-oval and narrow. The margin is almost straight and is sharp, with a distinct lip on its inner surface. The edges are joined together by a callus: the columellar edge is wide and open.

Colouring: milky white, tinged blue or light brown on the apex; the interior of the aperture is brown, the lip is white.

Size of shell: height 15—25 mm, width 5—6.5 mm.

Habitat: grassy hillsides with various types of vegetation on a dry, chalky substrate.

Distribution: endemic to the Black Sea coast of Bulgaria, extends to Dobrógea (Romania).

3. *Chondrus zebra tantalus* (L. PFEIFFER, 1868) — Pontic. The shell is cylindrically fusiform, thick-walled, glossy, opaque and sparsely but finely sculptured. It has 8—12 faintly convex, slowly growing whorls with a deep suture. The elongate-oval aperture has three lobes and three conspicuous teeth. The slightly widened margin has a flat lip on its inner surface.

Colouring: dingy white, generally with brown cross stripes.

Size of shell: height 8—17 mm, width 3—4 mm.

Habitat: dry grassy hillsides with low herbaceous vegetation.

Distribution: Serbia, Bulgaria (Rhodope), Greece and Turkey (central Anatolia).

Family: **Succineidae** — **Amber Snails**

These snails have a large body which cannot be withdrawn far into the shell. The lower pair of tentacles (characteristic of the order Stylommatophora) is vestigial. The shell is usually light brown, thin-walled, glossy and translucent, with a short spire and a relatively large expanded body whorl and aperture. The members of this family typically inhabit wet places and some are amphibious. They are distributed almost everywhere in the world. Specimens of Amber Snails sometimes need dissecting to confirm an identification on the shape of the jaw and character of the reproductive system.

1. *Succinea putris* (LINNAEUS, 1758), **Amber Snail** — Eurosiberian. The shell is pointedly ovoid, with a widened, bulging terminal whorl. It is thin-walled and highly translucent and its faintly glossy surface is irregularly marked with both fine and coarse grooving. Of the 3—4 whorls, the penultimate one is slightly convex and the last one, below the suture, is flat or slightly concave. The aperture is oval, with a distinct sharp angle at the top. The margin is straight and sharp and only the columellar segment is a little thicker. The parietal callus is thin, but clearly discernible. The shell is very variable, especially as regards its size; robust forms preponderate in damp, low-lying country, elsewhere smaller forms (under 18 mm) tend to be commoner.

Colouring: variable, from light greenish yellow to amber or dark orange.

Size of shell: height 16—22 mm, width 8—12 mm; the aperture accounts for about two thirds of the height of the shell.

Habitat: the banks of various types of water, mainly in lowlands, where the snail frequents rushes and leaves; it also is to be found — though less abundantly — in wet meadows and other damp places. *S. putris* goes further away from water than *Oxyloma elegans*. Finds in mountainous country are sporadic and chiefly comprise small forms; in the Alps they occur at altitudes of up to 1,800 m.

Distribution: appears in many forms throughout the whole of Europe and in western and northern Asia.

Succinea oblonga DRAPARNAUD, 1801. See p. 192.
Catinella arenaria (BOUCHARD—CHANTEREAUX, 1837). See p. 192.

2. *Oxyloma elegans* (RISSO, 1826) (= *O. pfeifferi*), **Pfeiffer's Amber Snail** — Palaearctic. The shell is slimly ovoid, thin-walled, but strong and highly transparent. The last of the $2^1/_2$—3 whorls is not so dilated as in the preceding species. The aperture is slender and oval and is pulled over to one side, so that its axis does not lie parallel to the axis of the shell. The margin is straight and sharp and is slightly thickened only on the columella. There are also differences in the genital apparatus and in the jaw when compared with *Succinea putris*. The body is often dark in colour in *O. elegans*.

Colouring: amber or dark yellow.

Size of shell: height 12—20 mm, width 6—9 mm; the aperture accounts for two thirds or more of the height of the shell.

Habitat: lives on reeds or in mud beside water, often in large numbers; is also to be found on objects floating on the water. It has a predilection for chalky lowlands.

Distribution: various forms inhabit the whole of Europe, north-west Africa and northern and western Asia.

Family: **Endodontidae**

Representatives of this large and ancient family are distributed all over the world. They have a small to moderately large and usually discoid shell with a wide, shallow umbilicus. The aperture is generally toothless. The snails inhabit damp, shady localities.

1. *Discus rotundatus* (MÜLLER, 1774), **Rounded Snail** — Subatlantic. The shell is markedly compact and convexly discoid, with relatively thin, but strong walls and a silky sheen. On its upper surface it is very regularly and densely ribbed; on its under side the ribbing is present but less evident. It is a tightly coiled shell with $5^1/_2$—$6^1/_2$ whorls which increase slowly in size; they are clearly convex and have a blunt, but very distinct ridge at the periphery. The aperture is an oblique, regularly transversal ellipse; the margin is sharp and straight or slightly blunted. The umbilicus is a deep and wide depression.

Colouring: the ground colour is a light greyish brown; on the whorls there are indistinctly circumscribed reddish brown spots occurring at fairly regular intervals. Sometimes unicoloured (with a whitish or greenish shell) and unspotted forms occur.

Size of shell: width 5.5—7 mm, height 2.4—2.8 mm.

Habitat: from lowlands to mountains (in the Alps up to 2,700 m), under stones, in rubble, beside tree trunks, under rotting wood and at the foot of rocks. It also thrives in secondary habitats, such as ruins, old garden walls, abandoned orchards and cemeteries.

Distribution: the whole of western and central Europe, the south of Scandinavia, eastwards (on a limited scale) to the western Carpathians and the Crimea. Absent in the south of Spain, on Sicily and on the Balkan peninsula.

2. *Discus ruderatus* (FÉRUSSAC, 1821) — Palaearctic (boreomontane). This has a similarly shaped shell to the preceding species, with thin, fragile walls and the same ribbing. Compared with *D. rotundatus* it is less tightly coiled with only 4—$4^1/_2$ whorls, which expand more rapidly, are fully convex and the body whorl of the adult has a rounded periphery without a ridge. The aperture is oblique and drawn somewhat downwards and sideways. The umbilicus is wide and open. Young specimens have a blunt, rounded ridge along their circumference.

Colouring: the shell is light greyish brown, greenish brown or reddish brown and — unlike *D. rotundatus* — always just the one colour.

Size of shell: width 5.5—6 mm, height 2.5—3 mm.

Habitat: this species inhabits damp mountain forests, generally above 800 m, where it is to be found behind the bark of rotting trunks and stumps (very often of fir-trees). It is a characteristic montane gastropod and lives in the Alps at altitudes of over 2,500 m; in some places it descends to the floor of deep valleys.

Distribution: the whole of northern Eurasia, the Alps, occasionally the Pyrenees, Germany, the Czech and Slovak Republics, Austria, Poland, Hungary, former USSR, Romania.

Family: **Arionidae — Slugs**

The family comprises robust slugs with a roughly tuberculate skin. The mantle shield or scutellum is rounded, both anteriorly and posteriorly, and the pneumostome or breathing pore lies at the anterior part of the lower right margin. There is no keel and the back and the posterior end or tail of the body are therefore rounded. The slugs are either unicoloured or have dark stripes on their sides. Their slime is very sticky; it can be coloured or colourless and it is secreted by a mucous gland situated above the tip of the rear end of the body. A rudiment of a shell is often present in the form of chalky granules below the mantle shield. Since some species look very much alike, the genital apparatus often has to be dissected to check the identification.

The family as a whole occurs throughout the Holarctic, but its typical genus, *Arion*, is to be found only in Europe. Its members are in general herbivorous, but they have omnivorous tendencies, also eating carrion: some of them are agricultural and horticultural pests.

Arion rufus (LINNAEUS, 1758), **Red Slug** — central European. The slug has a robust, long, wide body somewhat rounded and flattened at the back. If irritated, it contracts to a hemispherical shape and sways from side to side. The mantle shield is coarsely granular and the relatively long back and sides are covered with prominent tubercles. The respiratory orifice is strikingly large when it is opened.

Colouring: this species can be many-colours, but its back, sides and scutellum are usually of one colour (orange, light red, reddish brown, dark brown or black). The sole almost always has a reddish border or foot fringe marked with wide and narrow dark cross lines; the sole itself is grey. The slime on the upper surface of the body is stick; in reddish coloured animals it is orange, in brown and dark specimens colourless. The sole slime is colourless. Dark forms usually predominate in cold localities, brighter coloured forms in warm places.

Size: adult specimens measure 100—150 mm when stretched out full length and up to 80 mm when contracted.

Habitat: damp woods (especially greenwoods), sometimes thickets and meadows. This is a characteristic species of seaside woods, but it also invades cultivated country and gardens. It lives on both plant and animal food.

Distribution: the original area of this species includes central Europe and part of western Europe (France), where it adjoins the area of the closely related *Arion ater* (some authors regard the two slugs as subspecies of the same species). The *ater* and *rufus* forms are distinguished by features of the reproductive system. Its southernmost boundary are the Alps, while its eastern limits run through western Poland and Bohemia. In other parts of Europe it is an immigrant.

Lower part of the genital apparatus of *Arion rufus*

Family: **Arionidae — Slugs**

1. *Arion circumscriptus* JOHNSTON, 1828 — European. This slug has an elongate and dorsoventrally slightly flattened body.

Colouring: its back is steely blue to ash grey, but sometimes dark grey. The middle of its back and mantle shield are dark and in this ground colour we can see irregular black spots, which become more distinct after fixation, especially on the mantle. The lateral stripes are dark grey (sometimes almost black); they have a sharply defined upper margin, but their lower margin is indistinct because the pigmentation blends with the colouring of the sides, which below the stripes are therefore very dark. In live specimens the sole is milk white, in fixed specimens it is creamy white.

Size: full length the body can measure up to 40 mm, but mostly measures up to 25 mm; contracted it can measure up to 27 mm (usually 15—20 mm).

Habitat: damp mixed woods, particularly with alders. It mostly frequents small valleys and ravines, especially where there is an abundance of fallen leaves. This is a ground-dwelling slug and does not climb up tree trunks. It generally inhabits flat country; in the mountains it is succeeded by the related *A. silvaticus*, from which it differs in respect of the spots on its back and mantle, its dark sides and its blue-tinged colouring. *A. silvaticus* has pale sides.

Distribution: the west of the European part of the former USSR, Finland, Sweden, Poland, the Czech and Slovak Republics, the Netherlands, France. Other reported finds are not reliable, since this species is often confused with the similar *A. silvaticus* and *A. fasciatus*, which were all three once aggregated under the name *Arion circumscriptus*.

2. *Arion fasciatus* (NILSON, 1823), **Banded Slug** — European. A larger, distinctly flatter and wider species than *A. circumscriptus*.

Colouring: the body is always light-coloured, with a faded appearance. The ground colour is cream or ashy yellow. The middle of the back and the mantle are somewhat darker and are unspotted. The lateral stripes are dark grey, with a sharply defined upper and lower margin. In living specimens, faint, narrow yellow, orange or reddish lines and flecks can be seen below the dark stripes, but alcohol fixation causes them to disappear, together with the yellowish shade of the ground colour so that the body turns light grey. In living specimens the sole is creamy; after fixation it is white. The slime is usually colourless.

Size: fully extended the body measures up to 50 mm, contracted up to 32 mm.

Habitat: mainly cultivated localities, e. g. kitchen-gardens, parks, fields, old cemeteries, etc. The slug has a predilection for damp spots under shrubs and trees and wet meadows alongside rivers. It is active chiefly at night and spends the daytime hiding under stones, wood and other objects. It occurs together with the synanthropic species *Arion hortensis*, *Trichia hispida* and *Cepaea nemoralis*.

Distribution: it is evidently distributed throughout the whole of Europe and has also found its way to the USA.

Family: **Arionidae** — **Slugs**

1. *Arion subfuscus* (DRAPARNAUD, 1805), **Forest** or **Dusky Slug** — European. Seen from above, its elongate body has relatively parallel sides. The mantle shield (scutellum), which takes up about one third of the length of the body, is oval, with a widely rounded posterior end. The dorsal tubercles are thin and not as prominent as in *A. ater* and *A. rufus*; there are 19—20 between the midline and the pneumostome.

Colouring: very variable, both within the population and during the animal's lifetime. The shade of the ground colour varies from cinnamon brown to orange, but is most often russet or greyish cinnamon brown. The back is usually the darkest part and there are no distinctive lateral stripes. There are, however, specimens with bright stripes on their back and a lyre-shaped pattern on their mantle shield. These markings are most frequently found in young specimens and in the early phase of sexual activity. On the back they are often indistinct, but the respiratory orifice is encircled by dark pigment. The sole is always creamy. A distinctive feature of this slug is the tan-coloured slime produced from its mantle.

Size: full length 35—80 mm, contracted length up to 45 mm.

Habitat: various types of forests at low and high altitudes, also peat-bogs; less common in disturbed habitats. The slug lives on mushrooms, plants, carrion and the excreta of invertebrates.

Distribution: the European part of the former USSR and the Caucasus; otherwise practically the whole of Europe. Has also been carried to other parts of the world.

2. *Arion distinctus* MABILLE, 1868 — Holarctic (?).

Colouring: generally yellow-grey, the head and the tentacles bluish black or grey. The lateral stripes are situated relatively low on the body sides and at the rear end of the body they draw close and nearly touch in the front part enveloping thus the mantle shield; in the middle of the back at the rear end there is a fine yellow stripe.

Habitat: mostly man-made biotopes (gardens, parks, fields, etc.).

Distribution: Europe, North America. Detailed description only from Sweden, Germany, Austria. No exact description and distribution known in Europe due to the possible confusion with the similar species (*A. hortensis, A. owenii*) which were once included in the aggregate species *A. hortensis*.

Arion hortensis. FÉRUSSAC, 1819. See also p. 192.
Arion owenii DAVIES, 1979. See also p. 192.
Geomalacus maculosus (ALLMAN, 1843). See p. 193.

Family: **Vitrinidae — Glass Snails**

The shell is very thin, glossy and transparent and consists of a few rapidly expanding whorls. The aperture is usually extremely large and the umbilicus is generally missing. The body is large compared with the shell and in most species it cannot be fully retracted. In front of the shell and on the right side, the mantle forms fleshy lobes which sometimes cover the apex of the shell. This family occurs in the Holarctic region. Some species cannot be reliably identified from their external appearance, they differ only in their internal anatomy.

1. *Vitrina pellucida* (MÜLLER, 1774), **Pellucid Glass Snail** — Holarctic. The shell is a compressed sphere with a mildly prominent spire; it is very thin-walled, but relatively strong, is almost smooth and has a high gloss. The last of the 3—3^1/$_2$ rapidly growing whorls is slightly compressed at the aperture and makes up almost two fifths of the width of the shell. The aperture is oblique and is shortly elliptical or rounded. The margin is straight and sharp and the membranous (conchiolin) margin forms a narrow border along its lower edge. The animal can withdraw completely into its shell.

Colouring: the shell is glassy and usually pale green but may be colourless. The body is light grey, with a darker head, and this shows through the shell.

Size of shell: width 4.5—6 mm, height 3.4 mm.

Habitat: forests, valley vegetation and the banks of streams, but also well-covered grassy hillsides and rock rubble. Occurs in the Alps at altitudes of up to 3,100 m. Also common on cultivated land, e. g. in gardens and orchards, etc. Appears in large numbers in the autumn.

Distribution: the whole of Europe except the most southerly parts, inner and northern Asia, North America.

2. *Eucobresia diaphana* (DRAPARNAUD, 1805) — Alpine-central European. The shell is compressed, with auriculate contours, and has a slightly prominent spire; it is very thin-walled, fragile, almost smooth and highly lustrous. The last of the 2 ^{1}/$_2$ rapidly expanding whorls (body whorl) is compressed at the aperture and accounts for at least half of the width of the shell. The aperture is markedly oblique and transversely oval; the margin is straight. The membranous margin is wide and at its widest spot it makes up two fifths to half the width of the lower edge. The columella allows a view of the inside of the shell right up to the apex; there is no umbilicus. The animal is unable to withdraw completely into its shell.

Colouring: the shell is glassy, usually colourless, but often greenish. The animal itself is dark grey.

Size of shell: width 6—6.7 mm, height 3.2 mm.

Habitat: damp, cold places at both low and high altitudes, especially in valley vegetation or beside streams, etc. Ascends to 2,800 m in the Alps.

Distribution: the Alps, Germany, the Netherlands, Austria, the Czech and Slovak Republics, Poland, former Yugoslavia, Bulgaria.

Phenacolimax major (FÉRUSSAC, 1807). See p. 193.

Family: Zonitidae — Glass Snails

This family chiefly consists of small to moderately large snails with a flat, glossy and thin-walled shell. After death, the shell very soon turns white and opaque, so old shells may be difficult to identify. This large family is distributed over the whole of the northern hemisphere. Some species live underground and are partly or completely carnivorous. Many species are very hard to identify from the shell alone, so that it is often necessary to dissect the genital apparatus. European species belong to the genera *Vitrea, Aegopis, Nesovitrea, Aegopinella, Retinella, Oxychilus, Daudebardia* and *Zonitoides.*

1. *Aegopis verticillus* (FÉRUSSAC, 1822) — east Alpine-Dinarian. The shell is somewhat flattened and round, with a low conical spire and thick, slightly translucent walls; its upper surface is reticulated, while its under side is almost smooth and very glossy. It has 6—6 ^{1}/$_2$ whorls whose size increases gradually and regularly; the first four have a sharp peripheral keel, but the body whorl, at the aperture, is completely rounded. The aperture is slightly oblique and has a straight, sharp margin with a flat white lip. The wide and open — but deep — umbilicus accounts for about one fifth of the width of the shell.
Colouring: the upper surface is light greyish brown, the under side light yellowish grey with a greenish tinge. On the whorls, at irregular intervals, we can see 5—6 yellow cross bands, with a dark brown border in front; these are former positions of the lip which denote the individual growth stages and show through the shell.
Size of shell: width 26—30 mm, height 17 mm.
Habitat: preferably damp forests with a rubbly floor on a chalk or marl base. Occurs in the Alps at altitudes of up to 2,200 m.
Distribution: the north-western part of the Balkans, the eastern Alps. Austria, Germany, the Czech and Slovak Republics, Hungary.

2. *Aegopis acies* (FÉRUSSAC, 1819) — Dinarian. The shell has 6—7 whorls and a sharp peripheral keel on the body whorl.
Colouring: the upper surface is light brown or yellow, the keel is white.
Size of shell: width 30—33 mm, height 14 mm.
Habitat: damp forests with a rubbly floor on a chalky substrate.
Distribution: endemic to the western part of the Balkan peninsula.

3. *Aegopinella nitens* (MICHAUD, 1831) — Alpine-central European. The shell has 4^1/$_2$ whorls and in completely adult specimens the last quarter of the whorl is flattened (as distinct from the related *A. nitidula*) and sometimes curves slightly downwards. The umbilicus is wide.
Colouring: the shell is brown to greenish brown.
Size of shell: width 8—11 mm, height 3.5—4 mm.
Habitat: a mainly montane species living in forests among stones.
Distribution: chiefly the east of France, Switzerland, Germany, Austria, the Czech Republic, Slovakia and in parts of Poland and of former northern Yugoslavia.

Aegopinella nitidula (DRAPARNAUD, 1805). See p. 193.
Aegopinella pura (ALDER, 1830). See p. 193.

90

Family: **Zonitidae — Glass Snails**

1. *Oxychilus draparnaudi* (BECK, 1837). **Draparnaud's Glass Snail** — Atlantic-Mediterranean. The discoid shell has $5^1/_2$—6 whorls, the last one of which expands relatively quickly and is distinctly more expanded than in the closely related *O. cellarius*. The umbilicus is moderately deep and open. It has a slightly elevate spire.
Colouring: the shell is light olive brown, the animal itself blue-grey with a grey mantle.
Size of shell: width 11—16 mm, height 4.6—7 mm. Central European specimens are usually smaller than shells from western Europe.
Habitat: in its original area it lives among stones in damp, shady spots in woods and copses. In central Europe it frequents warmer (and hence drier) places.
Distribution: western and southern Europe. It follows in the wake of human settlements far inland, where it lives chiefly in gardens, on old walls and in greenhouses.

2. *Oxychilus deilus rumelicus* (HESSE, 1913) — Pontic. The shell is shaped like a compressed sphere, has a clearly discernible spire and is relatively strong. It has 6—$6^3/_4$ whorls; the first ones grow evenly, the last one more expanded; the body whorl is rounded and is 1 $^1/_2$ times wider than the penultimate whorl. The aperture is obliquely oval, the margin is sharp and the umbilicus is narrow, but deep.
Colouring: the upper surface of the shell is yellowish brown, the under side lighter.
Size of shell: width 13—17 mm, height 6.6—7.4 mm.
Habitat: it inhabits damp places and swamps and is to be found under rotting wood and leaves and in wet meadows.
Distribution: the southern and eastern part of Bulgaria and the Black Sea area of Turkey.

Oxychilus cellarius (MÜLLER, 1774), See p. 193.
Oxychilus alliarius (MILLER, 1822). See p. 194.
Oxychilus helveticus (BLUM, 1881). See p. 194.

3. *Zonitoides nitidus* (MÜLLER, 1774), **Shiny Glass Snail** — Holarctic. The shell is compressed and rounded, with a somewhat elevate spire; it is thin-walled and highly translucent. Its $4^1/_2$—5 mildly convex whorls grow slowly and regularly. The aperture is oblique and the margin is straight and sharp. The wide, open umbilicus takes up about one fifth of the shell diameter.
Colouring: the shell is a rich reddish brown (but may fade in empty shells). Since the animal itself is dark bluish grey the general colour effect is blackish brown. A yellow spot on the mantle shows through the shell just above the upper edge of the margin.
Size of shell: width 6—7 mm, height 3.5 mm.
Habitat: very damp marshes beside various types of water, in wet meadows, swamps and wet woods.
Distribution: practically the whole of Europe (absent over large parts of western Scandinavia), northern Asia and North America.

Zonitoides excavatus (ALDER, 1830). See p. 194.
Nesovitrea hammonis (STRÖM, 1765). See p. 194.

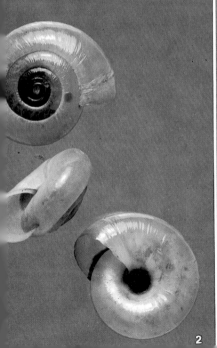

Family: **Euconulidae**

The members of this family have small, roundedly spherical shells, usually thin and glossy, with tightly coiled whorls. The aperture is thin with a simple margin. The umbilicus is small or completely closed. The various species live in damp localities; in Europe they are represented only by the genus *Euconulus*, which has a tightly coiled conical shell with a flat base; they are found in marshes and in leaf litter.

Family: **Limacidae—Keeled Slugs**

This family, which is distributed chiefly over the western part of the Palaearctic region, comprises slugs with an elongate body measuring anything from 45 to 200 mm. The granular or concentrically folded mantle shield or scutellum occupies one third of the length of the body and its anterior part covers the neck. The nucleus of the concentric folds is nearly central. The breathing pore or pneumostome is in the posterior half of the mantle shield on the right side. A relatively sharp keel runs part of the way along the back and the caudal or tail end of the slug is pointed. The sole is divided into three longitudinal, sharply circumscribed fields, the outer ones of which are sometimes darker than the middle one. The rudimentary shell, in the form of a flat chalky plate, is internal and lies within the mantle shield.

Bielzia coerulans (M. BIELZ, 1851) — Carpathian. This slug has a very robust body which tapers steadily, but sharply, towards its caudal end. The keel ends half to two thirds of the way along the dorsal midline. The mantle shield occupies less than one third of the length of the back and is posteriorly pointed. The dorsal dermal tubercles are very strongly developed, narrow and sharply prominent.

Colouring: very variable and dependent on the slug's growth and physiological condition. Adult specimens are grey, greyish green, bluish green, blue, dark violet or almost black. The keel is not distinctively coloured. The sole is either a uniform greyish black, or the outer fields are darker than the middle one. The slime is transparent and pale yellow. Blue colouring and blue shades do not appear until adulthood. Young specimens are differently coloured. They usually have an olive-tinged dark brown back with two dark brown stripes below the keel which sometimes stretch as far as the scutellum; their sides, keel and head are dark yellow and their sole is greyish green to yellow.

Size: fully extended the body measures up to 120 mm, contracted up to 90 mm.

Habitat: found in fairly warm and very damp mountain forests. The slug is particularly abundant and active during the daytime after summer rain, when it busily crawls about eating mushrooms, lichens, wild strawberries and — when all else fails — grass. Otherwise it hides under brushwood, bark, leaves and rotting tree trunks.

Distribution: the Czech and Slovak Republics, Poland, possibly Hungary, the Ukraine, Romania.

Euconulus fulvus (Müller, 1774) (2.9 × 2.3 mm)
Tawny Glass Snail

Family: Limacidae — Keeled Slugs

1. *Limax maximus* LINNAEUS, 1758, **Great Grey Slug** — south-west European. A large slug with a slender body and a keel occupying about one third of the body length. The dermal tubercles are long and elliptical, with a point at the front and the back. The mantle shield is rounded in front and pointed behind.
Colouring: very variable; usually light grey to whitish, less often dark grey. On the back and sides there are often two or three dark stripes or rows of spots. The mantle shield is usually irregularly marked with dark spots, but occasionally with faint lateral stripes. The keel and the unicoloured sole are light. The slime is thick and colourless.
Size: fully extended 100—200 mm, contracted up to 100 mm.
Habitat: Under natural conditions the slug usually inhabits greenwoods, mixed woods and thickets, where it hides under wood and stones. Among man-made habitats it occurs in parks, gardens, cellars, greenhouses, underground conduits and tunnels.
Distribution: the mountainous parts of western, southern and (in part) central Europe and North Africa are evidently its original area. It occurs as a synanthropic species over practically the whole of Europe, in particular the north and the east, and has also been introduced to the other continents.

2. *Limax cinereoniger* WOLF, 1803, **Ash-black Slug** — European. This species has a robust body with a thick keel which accounts for about half of the dorsal midline. It resembles the preceding species, but has a firmer skin and rougher, longer and narrower tubercles. It is also distinguished from *L. maximus* by the tripartite foot sole, which is dark at the edge and cream in the middle, and by black spots on its tentacles.
Colouring: varies with the locality, but also within the same population. Young specimens are usually light-coloured, creamy or cinnamon brown, with or without indistinct markings; the dark pigment on the sole appears later. The ground colour of adult individuals is white, grey, yellow and sometimes rusty brown. The markings on the back consist of three pairs of dark stripes or rows of spots. The mantle shield is always a uniform dark colour. The keel is lighter than the back. On the sole, the grey or black outer fields contrast sharply with the white middle field. Excessive production of dark pigment gives rise to black specimens.
Size: completely extended 150—200 mm, occasionally up to 300 mm; contracted up to 100 mm.
Habitat: mainly woods, but occasionally old parks, where the slug is to be found beside tree trunks, behind the bark of trees or stumps and under stones. It shuns cultivated country.
Distribution: in various parts of the whole of Europe except the extreme north.

3. *Limax cinereoniger*: eggs laid in woodland leaf litter.

Limax flavus (LINNAEUS, 1758). See p. 195.
Limax maculatus (KALENICZENKO, 1851). See p. 195.

Family: **Limacidae** — **Keeled Slugs**

1. *Lehmannia marginata* (MÜLLER, 1774) (= *Limax marginatus*), **Tree Slug** — European. This slug has a slender watery-looking body with a thin partly transparent skin. The mantle shield tapers off to a blunt point at the back; the keel is thin and short.

Colouring: the ground colour is grey, tinged with reddish brown, and a light stripe runs down the middle of the back. On the sides there are one or two pairs of stripes; the lower one is less distinct and often breaks up into a row of spots. The mantle shield always has lyriform markings and in the centre it also has a darker longitudinal field. The colour is variable and the markings may be absent. This species is distinguished from immature specimens of *Limax cinereoniger* and *L. maximus* mainly by its blood sinus and by its soft, flatly tuberculate skin, which becomes watery when irritated.

Size: Fully extended up to 75 mm, contracted up to 40 mm.

Habitat: lives only in natural habitats in lowlands and hilly country (in mixed woods and greenwoods, especially beechwoods). In damp weather or after dark it climbs up tree trunks right to the top, but in dry weather hides deep in crevices during daytime. It favours smooth-barked trees.

Distribution: practically the whole of Europe except the extreme north of Scandinavia and the southern Balkans; it extends eastwards to the western part of the former USSR.

2. *Malacolimax tenellus* (MÜLLER, 1774), **Slender Slug** — north to central European. The body is relatively small, very fine and translucent, with a soft skin and fine tubercles. The blunt keel is prominent only near the tail. The mantle shield takes up less than one third of the total length.

Colouring: the upper surface of the body is yellow, greenish yellow or greyish yellow (rarely yellowish orange). The head and tentacles are black or dark brown and the sole is light yellow or cream. After fixation a dark lyriform pattern, with a dark spot in the centre, appears on the mantle and dark longitudinal stripes can be seen on the back. Young specimens are usually lighter. The yellow pigment disappears soon after fixation and the body turns cream. The slime is watery and yellow.

Size: fully extended 25—50 mm, contracted 15—35 mm.

Habitat: this species lives mainly in forests at various altitudes; sometimes it occurs in old parks. Together with *Arion subfuscus*, it is one of the few gastropods to inhabit conifer plantations. Mushrooms and/or lichens are its staple diet; the young live on the mycelium. The slug attains sexual maturity at the end of the summer or the beginning of the autumn; after copulation it lays about 120 eggs, which are hatched the following year.

Distribution: occurs over large areas of central, western, north-western and northern Europe, except the most northerly parts.

1

2

Family: **Agriolimacidae — Field Slugs**

This family contains smaller species than the Limacidae family. The mantle shield covers the anterior half of the body and the extent of the keel is less. The nucleus of the concentric folds of the mantle shield is to one side and lies above the pneumostome. Most of the species can also be identified from their genital apparatus. The family is distributed over the entire Holarctic region, but is concentrated mostly in the Mediterranean and Black Sea countries.

1. *Deroceras reticulatum* (MÜLLER, 1774), **Grey Field Slug** — European. The slug is robustly built, with a wedge-shaped rear end and a markedly convex back. The mantle shield occupies about two fifths of the length of the body.

Colouring: the ground colour of adult specimens is dingy cream or pink, coffee or olive. There are usually distinct reticulate markings consisting of blackish or dark brown spots.

Size: fully extended 40—60 mm, contracted up to 25 mm.

Habitat: open spaces in cultivated country, where it lives wherever it is damp, e. g. under stones and wood, etc. This slug tends to avoid forests, but is a common field and garden pest.

Distribution: the whole of Europe as far as the Caucasus. Its natural area is undeterminable, because it often occurs by human habitations and in cultivated habitats and because, in the past, it was frequently confused with other related species.

Deroceras laeve (MÜLLER, 1774). See p. 195.
Deroceras caruanae POLLONERA, 1891. See p. 195.

Family: **Milacidae — Keeled Slugs**

This family includes robust slugs of various sizes, whose characteristic feature is a keel stretching, in most species, the full length of their back. The members of this family are closely related to the Limacidae family. They originally came from southern Europe; they are herbivorous and are sometimes pests: they do considerable damage to potato crops.

2. *Tandonia budapestensis* (HAZAY, 1881) (= *Milax budapestensis*), **Budapest Slug** —European. The slug has a moderately large body with a gradually tapering rear end. The mantle shield occupies about one quarter of its total length.

Colouring: its brown to yellowish grey-brown ground colour often darkens to grey or blackish brown on the back. The keel is yellow or orange, the dark-spotted mantle shield is largely devoid of pronounced lateral stripes and has a horse-shoe shaped indentation, the head is black and the yellowish white sole usually has a dark band in the middle. The slime is colourless, but irritation turns it yellow.

Size: fully extended 50—70 mm, contracted up to 40 mm.

Habitat: in its original habitats this slug lives in well-lit rubbly forests and on rocky hillsides with plenty of shrubs. It is a strongly synanthropic species, however, and in human settlements it occurs chiefly in parks and gardens and on piles of rubble. It is a pest in potato crops.

Distribution: its original area seems to have been southern Europe and some of the southern parts of central Europe; from here it has spread, through human agencies, to the rest of Europe.

Tandonia sowerbyi (FÉRUSSAC, 1823) (Milax). See p. 195.

Family: **Boettgerillidae**

Boettgerilla pallens SIMROTH, 1912. See p. 196.

Family: **Subulinidae**

The members of this family have a narrowly conical, pointed shell composed of a large number of whorls; the aperture is comparatively large. They live almost entirely in the tropics and except for a few greenhouse immigrants there is only one European member of the family.

1. *Rumina decollata* (LINNAEUS, 1758) — Mediterranean. Adult specimens have a cylindrical, thick-walled, opaque and slightly polished shell with 3—6 whorls, the oldest ones of which have broken away leaving a decollate spire which is plugged by a chalky secretion. Young shells are slim and pointed, with a bluntly rounded, hooked tip. A particular feature of this species is the ability to shed the apical whorls of the shell as soon as it has reached a given size; they do this about four times during their lifetime.
Colouring: the shell is light brown or cream, with a white lip but old shells bleach white.
Size of shell: height 22—35 mm, width 10—15 mm. Its size varies according to the type of environment (cultivated country, steppe or semi-desert).
Habitat: dry, open localities, grassy slopes, thickets, generally on chalky soil. To aestivate, the snails retire underground, under stones and into rock fissures.
Distribution: Mediterranean.

Family: **Clausiliidae — Door Snails**

The shell is generally sinistral, medium sized, often ribbed and fusiform or spindle-shaped, with a tapering spire formed of a large number of whorls. The aperture is relatively small and pear-shaped and inside it there is a variable and intricate complex of small teeth, folds and lamellae which are only partly visible from the outside. The species of this family inhabit the western part of the Palaearctic region, South America and south-eastern Asia. At least 150 species and a quantity of subspecies have been described in Europe (primarily in eastern Europe, in the Balkan countries and the Caucasus); westwards from the Balkans the number of clausiliid species diminishes. The snails live mainly in forests and among rocks; they normally hide in crevices, behind bark or in fallen leaves, but at night and in damp weather they crawl up the rocks or trees in search of algae and lichens. The shells of adult specimens are often whitish and corroded, or are covered with a greenish algal film.

2. *Agathyla exarata* (ROSSMÄSSLER, 1835) — an endemic species. The shell is cylindrically fusiform, fairly thin-walled, dull and sharply and conspicuously ribbed. It has 11—13 whorls and a highly compressed neck. The aperture is roundly pear-shaped; the margin is continuous, curved, sharp-edged and fragile.
Colouring: the ground colour is greyish violet, the ribbing white.
Size of shell: height 20 mm, width 3 mm.
Habitat: limestone rocks.
Distribution: endemic to Dalmatia (the valley of the river Neretva) and Herzegovina.

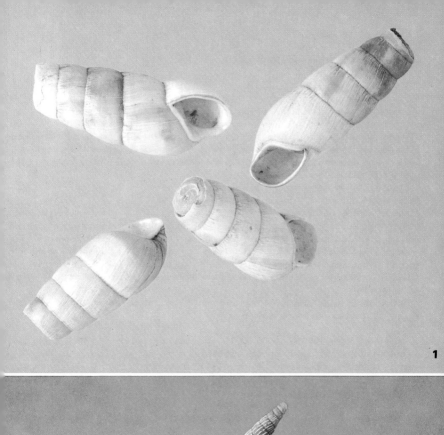

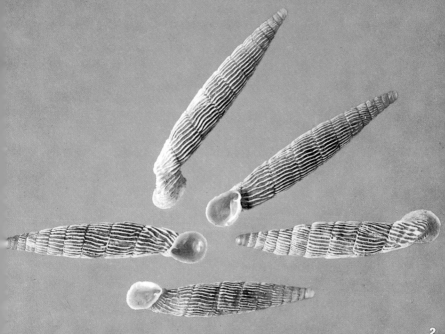

Family: **Clausiliidae — Door Snails**

1. *Herilla bosniensis* (L. PFEIFFER, 1868) — Dinarian. The moderately large shell has a swollen spindle-shaped form with ten whorls; it is practically smooth and is strong. The anterior surface is glossy and its posterior surface almost dull. The aperture is oval; the margin is joined together and is only slightly widened. Teeth: the superior lamella generally projects beyond the spiral lamella; the inferior lamella is high and forms no folds. Differences between the species and races of the genus *Herilla* can be determined primarily from the construction of the plate known as the clausilium inside the aperture.
Colouring: brownish violet or brownish red; the dorsal surface is lighter.
Size of shell: height 22—29 mm, width 6—7 mm.
Habitat: most of the species of the genus *Herilla* inhabit high, steep and light limestone cliffs, usually facing east or north. Sufficient atmospheric humidity is an essential condition and, in consequence, almost all low-lying localities are in the vicinity of rivers (e. g. in ravines). At higher altitudes (up to 1,800 m) the snails live further away from flowing water. It was in such ideal localities that the largest Clausiliidae species evolved, such as the closely related *Herilla illyrica,* whose shell is 36 mm tall.
Distribution: in Austria (near Vienna) and more commonly in Bosnia, Montenegro and Serbia, where it forms about ten races.

2. *Alopia plumbea* (ROSSMÄSSLER, 1839) — an endemic species. The shell is sinistral, swollen and fusiform, fairly smooth and fairly glossy with 10—13 whorls. The aperture is roundly pear-shaped; the margin is continuous, curves slightly outwards, away from the shell, and has a clearly discernible white lip.
Teeth: the superior lamella is long and not very prominent, while the inferior lamella is curved and very thick.
Colouring: according to the locality, the colour of the shell varies from light yellowish brown with a bluish tinge to blue-tinted reddish brown or deep bluish violet; the suture is white. The animal has an extremely granular back, which in light-coloured specimens is yellowish brown to greyish brown, with a light sole, and in dark individuals is brownish black with a yellowish grey sole.
Size of shell: height 17—26 mm, width 4.7—5.2 mm.
Habitat: Secondary (Jurassic) limestone rocks and conglomerate deposits overgrown with algae and lichens. In dry weather the snails collect in large numbers in fissures in the rocks.
Vertical distribution: 600—1,000 m.
Distribution: Romania — endemic to the northern part of the Bucegi Mountains (southern Carpathians) near Brasov.

Closure apparatus of species of the genus *Herilla* (view of the neck part)

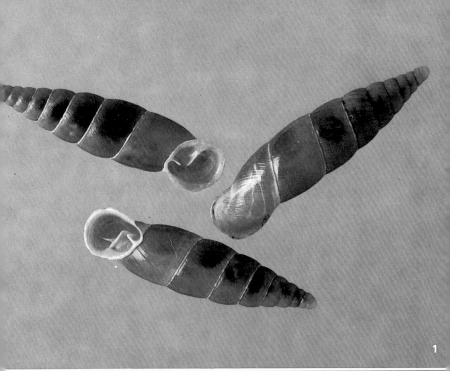

Family: **Clausiliidae — Door Snails**

1. *Alopia clathrata* (ROSSMÄSSLER, 1857) — an endemic species. The fusiform, dextral and dull shell is sculptured with conspicuous, widely spaced, blunt ribs, which are particularly irregular on the last of the $9-9^1/2$ whorls. The aperture is obliquely oval and has no basal groove. The very wide margin has a well developed white lip. The umbilicus is enclosed.

Teeth: the rather thick superior lamella does not stretch to the edge of the margin, the spiral lamella is separate and simple, the inferior lamella plunges quickly into the aperture, the subcolumellar lamella can hardly be seen from in front and on the palate there are three folds of almost equal thickness.

Colouring: the shell is light brown with a greyish tinge.

Size of shell: height $12-15$ mm, width $3.5-3.8$ mm.

Habitat: on sunny or partly shaded limestone cliffs; in dry weather the snails hide in crevices in the rocks.

Distribution: endemic to the Slovakian karst.

2. *Alopia cyclostoma albicostata* KIMAKOWICZ 1894 — an endemic species with a sinistral and a conical, rather than a fusiform, shell. Of the $9-10$ only slightly convex whorls, the penultimate one is the widest; the last one, with the umbilicus, is blunted at the bottom and is strikingly ribbed, paler ribs contrasting with the darker shell. The aperture is rounded and forms an angle only alongside the superior lamella. The margin is slightly thickened and spreading and is lined with a thick, white lip. Teeth: the superior lamella is very short and small, the inferior lamella can hardly be seen.

Colouring: the shell is brownish red to violet, with white ribs. The animal is greyish black.

Size of shell: height $12.8-16.4$ mm, width $3.6-4.5$ mm.

Habitat: limestone slopes facing south.

Distribution: endemic to the southern Carpathians (Bucegi, Romania).

3. *Alopia livida* (MENKE, 1830) — an endemic species. The shell is dextral, fusiform, finely grooved, glossy, thick-walled and opaque. The last of the $9-10$ mildly convex whorls bulges. The aperture is broadly oval and somewhat wider at the bottom. The margin is continuous and is pinched together at the top; it curves outwards and is lined with a clearly visible (and often completely white) lip. Teeth: the superior lamella is small and does not reach the edge of the margin; the large inferior lamella is curved in the shape of a letter S and is very prominent.

Colouring: the shell is dark violet with a greyish overtone, the suture and keel are white and the margin is brownish white. The animal is greyish black.

Size of shell: height $12-21$ mm, width $3.5-5$ mm.

Habitat: limestone rocks.

Distribution: endemic to the northern spurs of the Bucegi Mountains (southern Carpathians), where it ascends to altitudes of 2,600 m. Hungary and Germany (rare).

Family: **Clausiliidae — Door Snails**

1. *Medora contracta* (ROSSMÄSSLER, 1842) — Dinarian. The shell is moderately large, protuberantly fusiform and generally smooth, except for the neck (the back of the lower part of the shell), which is very coarsely ribbed. It is sinistral and the tapering spire has 8—9 whorls. The aperture is large and rounded; the spreading margin almost always stands out from the shell.
Colouring: the shell is whitish blue; the inside of the aperture is a bright yellowish brown.
Size of shell: height 16—27 mm, width 5—8 mm.
Habitat: as for the genus *Herilla*, beside rivers, lakes or the sea; inland, at higher altitudes, prefers south-facing rock walls. Most of its localities lie at altitudes of 0 to 1,000 m, but isolated finds are known at up to 1,900 m. The area of this species is mostly made up of single, isolated localities.
Distribution: Dalmatia, Herzegovina and Montenegro, where it forms two races.

2. *Albinaria inflata* (OLIVIER, 1801) — an endemic species. The shell is almost cylindrically fusiform, with 12—14 very slightly convex whorls, of which the upper ones are finely grooved, the middle ones smooth and the largest or body whorl bears pronounced nodose folds and — at the bottom — an inconspicuous keel. The aperture is oval and more or less vertical; the margin is sharp, everted and continuous.
Teeth: a small superior lamella, a deeply situated, but large inferior lamella.
Colouring: chalky white or bluish white, unicoloured or spotted; the interior of the aperture is bright brown.
Size of shell: height 21—23 mm, width 4—5 mm.
Habitat: damp rock walls in river valleys, old marble quarries, ancient ruins, stony places in general. Not all the members of the genus *Albinaria* (about 60 species and 200 races) require a chalky substrate (Triassic limestone, volcanic tuffs); they can also live on crystalline rocks.
Distribution: Greece — endemic to Crete.

3. *Sericata sericata* (L. PFEIFFER, 1849) — an endemic species. The shell is clavately fusiform and densely grooved, with a 10- to 11-whorl spire and a deep, thread-like suture. The last whorl is very low and has a faintly nodose keel at the bottom. The aperture is large and rounded; the margin projects a little way and then spreads out. In the centre of the parietal wall there are often a few irregular callus-like folds.
Teeth: the superior lamella is long, the inferior lamella is poorly developed.
Colouring: the shell is dark reddish brown or violet brown, with a white suture.
Size of shell: height 19—22 mm, width 4—5 mm.
Habitat: rocks.
Distribution: Greece, endemic to the northern and central part of Euboea (Évvoia).

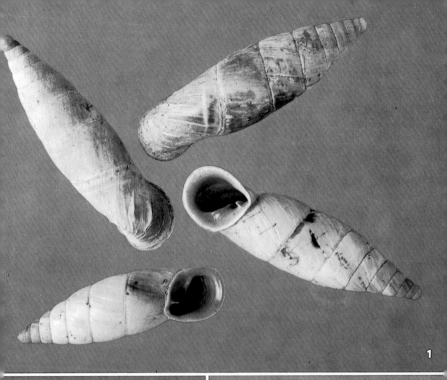

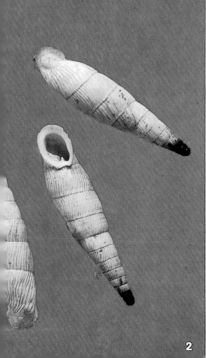

Family: Clausiliidae — Door Snails

1. *Macedonica frauenfeldi* (ROSSMÄSSLER, 1856) — Balkan. The shell is protuberantly fusiform and glossy; the upper whorls and the neck are finely ribbed. There are 10—11 faintly convex, very slowly expanding whorls. The aperture is oval to pear-shaped and is higher than it is wide; the margin is attached, thickened and everted.
Colouring: yellowish brown to violet brown with a blue overtone; the pronounced thread-like suture is white and the interior of the aperture is brown.
Size of shell: height 17—20 mm, width 4—5 mm.
Habitat: lives on limestone rocks and under stones.
Distribution: forms five races in the eastern part of Serbia and the western part of the Balkan Mountains (Bulgaria).

2. *Itala pfeifferi* (KÜSTER, 1847) — an endemic species. The shell is protuberantly fusiform, almost smooth and translucent, with hardly any gloss. The moderately long spire tapers off gradually to a blunt point. It has ten almost flat whorls; the upper ones are narrow, the lower ones relatively high and at the base of the body whorl, which is anteriorly grooved, there are two bosses separated by a wide, flat furrow. The aperture is wide and squatly pear-shaped; the margin is prominent and continuous and has a brownish white lip.
Colouring: violet brown with a white, thread-like suture; greyish red inside the aperture.
Size of shell: height 17—20 mm, width 4—4.5 mm.
Habitat: karst territory with greenwoods and mixed woods. Large populations are determined by a chalky substrate, high temperatures and a heavy rainfall.
Distribution: central Dalmatia.

3. *Charpentieria ornata* (ROSSMÄSSLER, 1836) — north-eastern Alpine. The shell is slimly fusiform, strong, translucent and faintly glossy. On the upper whorls there is fairly regular fine ribbing; the ribbing on the last two or three whorls is much less distinct and just below the suture some of the ribs terminate in whitish papillae, which follow the course of the suture at fairly regular intervals. In all, there are ten very slightly convex whorls. The relatively large aperture is obliquely pear-shaped and rounded at the bottom. The wide margin has a whitish lip and its edges are not joined together on the parietal segment. The parietal callus is well developed; the large, whitish palatal callus lies almost parallel with the margin.
Colouring: light brown with a faint reddish tinge, with striking white papillae below the suture and a brownish yellow-white nuchal callus.
Size of shell: height 15—18 mm, width 3.9—4.5 mm.
Habitat: limestone rocks, old ruins.
Distribution: the north-eastern Alps and the adjoining mountains. Austria, the Czech Republic, rarely Poland.

Family: **Clausiliidae** — **Door Snails**

1. *Cochlodina laminata* (MONTAGU, 1803), **Plaited Door Snail** — European. The shell is broadly fusiform and somewhat translucent, with fine, irregular grooving, but almost smooth shiny lower whorls. There are 11—12 faintly convex whorls. The aperture is squarely pear-shaped and has no basal groove. The margin is slightly widened and has a white lip; on the parietal wall the edges are joined together almost completely by a callus.
Colouring: yellowish brown to reddish brown.
Size of shell: height 15—17 mm, width 4 mm.
Habitat: woods at all altitudes; from lowland valley woods and warm, sheltered copses to virgin conifer forests in the mountains. Generally to be found beside tree trunks and behind bark; in damp weather climbs trees. In the Alps occurs at altitudes of up to 1,900 m.
Distribution: common throughout practically the whole of Europe.

2. *Balea biplicata* (MONTAGU, 1803), **Two-lipped Door Snail** — central European. The shell is slimly to broadly fusiform, strong, translucent and regularly ribbed, with 12—13 whorls. The aperture is lozenge- to pear-shaped, with a pronounced basal furrow and very distinct internal grooving. The margin is very wide, with a curved edge and a relatively thick whitish lip. On the neck there is a clearly discernible crest and furrow.
Colouring: light brown.
Size of shell: height 16—18 mm, width 3.8—4 mm. A very variable species with a whole series of forms.
Habitat: forest, where it lives beside trees, in rubble and on rocks, in valleys and on slopes and hill-tops. It also occurs in lowland riparian woods and invades man-made habitats (gardens, parks, cemeteries, ruins).
Distribution: the whole of central Europe — in the east to the western Carpathians, Hungary, Poland and the Czech and Slovak Republics, in the west to the north-east of France, Belgium, the Netherlands, Germany and Switzerland, in the south to the northern part of the Balkans, and in the north to England, Denmark, southern Norway and Sweden.

3. *Laciniaria plicata* (DRAPARNAUD, 1801) — central European. The shell is slimly fusiform, with 12—13 whorls and dense, regular ribbing. It resembles the shell of the preceding species, but on the margin of the aperture there are 6—9 thick folds, which may occasionally be reduced or missing. In the interlamellar space (interlamellare) there are two or three folds.
Colouring: light brown; along the suture the ribs are often white.
Size of shell: height 15—18 mm, width 3.3—3.6 mm.
Habitat: mainly damp rocks (particularly marl) and exposed ruins, less often woods on a chalky substrate, where it lives beside trees. In the Alps it occurs at altitudes of up to 2,300 m.
Distribution: the north-east of France, Austria and Switzerland, scattered incidences in the smaller mountains of Germany, Bohemia and Moravia, in the Carpathians, the west of the European part of the former USSR, the northern Balkans, northern Italy.

Family: **Clausiliidae — Door Snails**

1. *Erjavecia bergeri* (ROSSMÄSSLER, 1836) — east Alpine. A species easily identified from the unusual triangular shape of the aperture. The shell is smooth and dull and has ten whorls. The lip is wide and thick. In a vertical view of the shell, the inferior lamella can hardly be seen in the aperture.

Colouring: normally reddish brown, the shell acquires a bluish grey tinge if slightly weathered or if covered with fine calcified algae.

Size of shell: height 10.5—11.5 mm, width 2.3—2.5 mm.

Habitat: a calcicolous species inhabiting rock faces, it is the only east Alpine door snail which tolerates direct sunshine. It lives on cliffs or rocks which face south and are exposed for long periods to the sun. The snails like to cling, upside down, to overhanging rocks. Their vertical distribution ranges from 400 to 2,300 m.

Distribution: Austria, particularly Salzburg and the Salzkammergut region (upper Austria), and a few localities in Carinthia (the southern limestone Alps).

2. *Macrogastra ventricosa* (DRAPARNAUD, 1801) — European. The largest member of the genus *Macrogastra*. The shell is fusiform (often somewhat claviform), strong, fairly translucent, slightly glossy and regularly and relatively densely and deeply grooved, with 11—12 slightly convex whorls. The aperture is rectangularly elliptical, with a faint trace of a basal groove, which does not reach the margin. The margin is wide and everted, with a whitish lip; it stands away from the aperture and is continuous. Teeth: the fairly low superior lamella terminates on the margin and is joined to the spiral lamella. The inferior lamella is situated deeper in the aperture; one fold leads obliquely upwards from it to the margin, while another, thicker columellar fold leads inwards, so that the lamella looks like a sloping letter K. The subcolumellar lamella is only just visible from in front and is situated high up in the aperture; the interlamellare is smooth.

Colouring: reddish brown.

Size of shell: height 16—20 mm, width 4—4.5 mm. A relatively stable species, which only here and there, in inclement (particularly mountain) habitats, appears in a short, stunted form.

Habitat: damp upland and mountain forests, where it lives under fallen leaves, timber and mossy stones, together with the common *Macrogastra plicatula*. It avoids lowlands and warm unforested regions. In the Alps it ascends to 1,800 m.

Distribution: from the east of France to the west of the European part of the former USSR, the northern Carpathians, the Alps and their south-eastern spurs as far as the northern part of the Balkans, France, Belgium, Switzerland, Germany, Denmark, southern Scandinavia, Austria, Poland, the Czech and Slovak Republics, Hungary, the Ukraine, former Yugoslavia and Bulgaria.

The genus *Macrogastra* is represented in Britain by one species *M. rolphii* (TURTON 1826) that has a limited distribution in S. E. England but is widespread in France.

1

2

Family: **Clausiliidae — Door Snails**

1. *Vestia gulo* (BIELZ, 1859) — Carpathian. The shell is broadly fusiform, strong, slightly translucent, fairly glossy and regularly and fairly coarsely ribbed; it has 10 or 11 slightly convex whorls. The oblique aperture is squatly or roundly pear-shaped, with a relatively poorly developed basal groove. It has a very wide, prominent and continuous margin with a large whitish or pinkish lip. Teeth: the superior lamella is large, the spiral lamella is separate or joined to it by a low ridge, the inferior lamella usually (but not always) has one or two folds leading to the margin and the interlamellare is smooth. The subcolumellar lamella terminates in a small fold leading to the margin. On the palate there is a whitish callus, whose lower part is particularly thick and which almost unites with the lip.
Colouring: very light brown.
Size of shell: height 15—19 mm, width 4.3—4.9 mm.
Habitat: damp mountain forests, under stones and rotting vegetation. Has a predilection for marshy ground and the surrounds of springs.
Distribution: the Carpathians and adjoining mountains – in the west including Moravia and Slovakia, Poland and Hungary.

2. *Vestia turgida* (ROSSMÄSSLER, 1836) — Carpathian. The shell is bulkily fusiform, with a relatively slender apex; it is strong, markedly translucent, very glossy and both finely and coarsely grooved, although the last whorls are often almost smooth; in all, there are 10 or 11 whorls. The aperture is oblique and squatly or roundly pear-shaped, with a relatively poorly developed basal groove. The very wide margin has a thick, whitish lip which almost unites with the narrow palatal callus.
Teeth: the inferior lamella tapers off on the margin into one or two folds and there are sometimes folds on the interlamellare; the subcolumellar lamella leads almost to the margin, but is not actually visible from front. On the neck there is a very thin crest and an often indistinguishable furrow.
Colouring: reddish to yellowish brown, sometimes with a greenish tinge.
Size of shell: height 14—16 mm, width 3.6—3.9 mm. A very variable species, particularly as regards size and surface structure.
Habitat: similar localities to the preceding species. It likes damp valley bottoms with luxuriant vegetation and marshy sites in forests, but also occurs in drier localities.
Distribution: a large part of the Carpathian region; relict incidences further west, in the region of the adjoining Bohemian and Bavarian forests. A few parts of the Czech and Slovak Republics, southern Poland and northern Hungary.

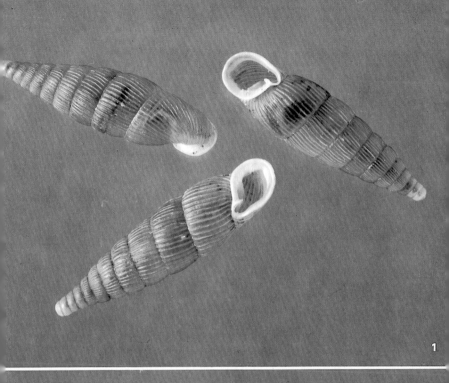

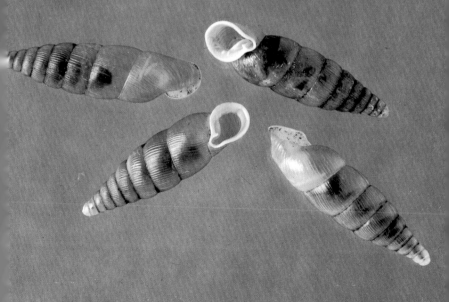

1

2

Family: **Clausiliidae** — **Door Snails**

1. *Clausilia dubia* DRAPARNAUD, 1805, **Craven Door Snail** — central European. The shell is both slimly and broadly fusiform, with 10—11¹/₂ whorls; it is fairly strong, somewhat translucent and finely and regularly ribbed with spiral lines. The aperture is pear- or lozenge-shaped. The fairly wide margin has a white lip. This very variable species forms many geographical races.
Colouring: the shell is dark reddish brown.
Size of shell: height 11—16 mm, width 2.7—3.2 mm.
Habitat: damp rocks and ruins, also woods (beside trees); most abundant on a chalky substrate. Occurs in the Alps at up to 2,400 m.
Distribution: from the Pyrenees to the Baltic countries in the east and in the northwestern Balkans; elsewhere only sporadic. France, Switzerland, Austria, Hungary, the Czech and Slovak Republics, Poland, Germany, Belgium, Netherlands, Norway, Sweden and British Isles.

Clausilia bidentata (STRÖM, 1765). See p. 196.

2. *Balea perversa* (LINNAEUS, 1758), **Tree Snail** — Atlantic-Mediterranean. The shell is narrowly conical, with thin, fragile walls and very fine, dense and almost regular ribbing; it has 9—10 whorls. The aperture, which is pear-shaped to oval, deviates a little to one side; it is toothless, or has only a very small parietal tooth. The margin is not very wide and has only a small white lip; it is joined together weakly on the parietal wall but does not project from the shell.
Colouring: light brown to yellowish.
Size of shell: height 8—10 mm, width 2.3 mm.
Habitat: a characteristic species of warm dry microhabitats among stones and in ruins; less common on trees, rare in fallen leaves.
Distribution: from Italy to the Iberian Peninsula and the whole of western Europe, north of this region as far as Great Britain and Scandinavia. Only scattered incidences in the mountains of central Europe.

Family: **Ferussaciidae**
These snails have a small, light-coloured, translucent and usually slimly fusiform shell with a simple, thin margin. They chiefly inhabit warm regions all over the world and since they live underground they are often blind, lacking eye spots.

Family: **Testacellidae** — **Shelled Slugs**
This family consists of slugs with a small external shell at the rear end of the body. They occur in the western Mediterranean region and along the Atlantic coast. They are carnivorous (eating earthworms), are very agile and are to be found mainly in cultivated habitats where they burrow under ground.

Family Ferussaciidae
Cecilioides acicula (Müller, 1774)
(5 × 1.2 mm)
Blind Snail
This is often found in ant-hills.

Testacella haliotidea Draparnaud, 1801
(body length 80—120 mm)
Shelled Slug

Family: **Oleacinidae**

Most of the members of this family inhabit tropical America, but *Poiretia* is a Mediterranean genus whose species are predacious and live mainly on other gastropods.

1. *Poiretia cornea* BRUMATI, 1838 — Dinarian. The shell is a tapering, thin-walled cone with $5^1/_2$ — $6^1/_2$ mildly convex, rapidly expanding whorls and a large aperture. The 2 — $2^1/_2$ larval whorls have a thread-like suture. The first whorl is completely smooth; the others are finely grooved.
Colouring: pale dingy yellow.
Size of shell: height 33 — 46 mm, width 10 — 16 mm.
Habitat: the same as for *Rumina decollata* and *Pomatias elegans*, which, together with earthworms, constitute its staple diet as a carnivore.
Distribution: from the northern shores of the Adriatic to the north of Albania and the Gargano peninsula (Italy).

Family: **Bradybaenidae**

This chiefly Asian family has only one species occurring in Europe.

2. *Bradybaena fruticum* (MÜLLER, 1774), **Bush Snail** — European. The strong, spherical shell has a widely conical spire; its 5 — $6^1/_2$ highly convex whorls increase regularly and fairly rapidly in size. The aperture is somewhat oblique; the margin is slightly widened and relatively sharp, with a poorly developed lip. The umbilicus is open and moderately wide.
Colouring: the shell is greyish white, yellowish, flesh-coloured or light reddish brown, sometimes with a brown peripheral band.
Size of shell: width 13—23 mm, height 10—19 mm.
Habitat: copses, bases of rock outcrops in forests, riparian lowlands; occurs secondarily in shrubs, on balks and in ditches.
Distribution: eastern France, Switzerland, Germany, Austria, the Czech and Slovak Republics, Poland, Hungary, Belgium, the Netherlands, Denmark, Norway, Sweden, Finland, former Yugoslavia, Bulgaria, Romania, the Ukraine, Crimea, the Caucasus.

Family: **Sphincterochilidae**

The members of this family have a massive, rounded or compressed shell with an oblique aperture. A few species live only in the Mediterranean region.

3. *Albea candidissima* (DRAPARNAUD 1801) (= *Sphincterochila candidissima*) — Mediterranean. The spherical, almost smooth, dull-surfaced and thick shell has 5—6 rapidly expanding whorls. The upper whorls are rather flat and have a keel; the last one is rounded and generally faintly angular. The aperture is deeply crescent-shaped; the margin is blunt and slightly widened. In adulthood the umbilicus is closed; in young specimens it is open when the shell also has a sharp keel.
Colouring: dingy white (in adult specimens chalky white).
Size of shell: width 16—22 mm, height 12—18 mm.
Habitat: it inhabits grassy hills near the coast and also inland, but prefers bare rocky mountains and stony hilltops.
Distribution: the south of France, Spain, Italy, Mediterranean islands and North Africa, continuing to Syria.

Family: **Helicidae**

Shells small to large (5—50 mm), often thick. The shape varies from discoidal through subglobular to globular and there is much variation between species in the numbers of whorls and in the proportion of the shell occupied by the body whorl. Juveniles are often slightly keeled, a feature usually lost in the adult. The shell lip is often thickened and reflected and there may be an internal rib inside it in the adult shells of some genera. The surface is only heavily sculptured in some genera (eg *Candidula*) while others exhibit periostracal hairs. Shell colour is variable — many are brown or white but some are more colourful (pink or yellow).

A very large family of common European snails with a greater number of species in the south of the region. This large family is further subdivided into subfamilies.

1. *Helicella itala* (LINNAEUS, 1758), **Heath Snail** — west European. The rounded, compressed shell has a low, flatly conical spire. It is strong, rather chalky, faintly translucent with fine and irregular growth lines and consists of $5^1/_2 — 6^1/_2$ convex and relatively slowly growing whorls. On reaching the aperture, the suture drops suddenly and rather abruptly downwards. The aperture is oblique and is rounded or transversely elliptical; on the parietal wall its edges come very close together. The margin is sharp; laterally, inferiorly and on the columellar segment it is distinctly widened, with a very thin lip. The wide, open umbilicus, a distinguishing feature, occupies almost one third of the width of the shell.

Colouring: the yellowish white or flesh-coloured shell is marked with translucent light or dark brown spiral bands; sometimes the bands almost disappear and occasionally they are absent altogether.

Size of shell: width 15—16 mm, height 6.5—7.5 mm.

Habitat: grassy hillsides, fields on a chalky substrate, road and railway embankments; in the Alps and Pyrenees up to 2,000 m.

Distribution: the whole of western Europe, the southern part of the British Isles part of the western Alps, the Jura Mountains; Germany, Austria, the Czech Republic.

2. *Helicella obvia* (MENKE, 1828) — east sub-Mediterranean. The 5—6 convex whorls increase regularly and quickly in size; the shallow suture, at the aperture slopes gently and steadily downwards. The white, wide, flat and slightly elevated lip is situated deep inside the aperture. The umbilicus takes up about one quarter of the width of the shell.

Colouring: dark brown to black bands on a white ground. The bands often split up unite or disintegrate; sometimes they are completely absent and sometimes the dominate the ground colour.

Size of shell: very variable; width 10.5—20 mm, height 5—10 mm.

Habitat: dry grassy hillsides, fields and baulks on chalky ground; in cold region only on limestone substrates. Secondarily colonizes road and railway embankment and ditches, etc.

Distribution: extends westwards from the Black Sea region to former Yugoslavia, Hungar Austria, Switzerland, Germany, the Czech and Slovak Republics.

Family: **Helicidae**

1. *Helicopsis striata* (MÜLLER, 1774) — central European. The shell is subglobular with a widely conical, elevated spire and fairly thick walls. It is strong, opaque, dull and irregularly sculptured with thick, blunt ribs. The last of the $4^1/2$ — 5 convex, evenly growing whorls clearly dominates the rest. The aperture slants a little and is rounded. The margin is sharp and straight; its lower and columellar segment may be very slightly widened. The whitish lip (situated inside the aperture of the adult shell) is flat, wide and thick. The open umbilicus is not very wide and takes up one seventh to one fifth of the width of the shell.

Colouring: on a whitish ground there are 1 — 8 dark brown bands, which often break up into rows of spots, merge or disappear; sometimes the shell is brown or pure white.

Size of shell: width 6 — 11 mm, height 4 — 6.5 mm.

Habitat: chiefly original grassy hillsides on an unconsolidated substrate (mainly windblown sand) at low altitudes.

Distribution: reliable data from France, Germany, Poland, the Czech and Slovak Republics, Hungary, Austria in the Vienna basin.

2. *Trochoidea elegans* (GMELIN, 1791), Top Snail — west Mediterranean. Since the under side is almost flat, the shell looks like a cone. It is densely and finely grooved and has 6 — 7 whorls with a sharp peripheral keel. The aperture is extremely flattened and on its outer surface is a sharp incision made by the peripheral keel. The margin is straight and sharp and inside it is a clearly discernible white lip. The umbilicus is small and circular.

Colouring: the shell is white or yellowish; it is either unicoloured or has a single brown stripe right up to the apex.

Size of shell: width 7 — 12 mm, height 5 — 9 mm.

Habitat: dry and open grassy localities in coastal regions — steppes, hillsides, dunes.

Distribution: the south-west of France, Spain, the Balearic Islands and North Africa. Limited introductions to Britain (near Dover).

3. *Trochoidea pyramidata* (DRAPARNAUD, 1805) — Mediterranean. The shell is bluntly conical, strong, opaque and finely grooved; it is tightly coiled and the blunt-tipped spire rises in steps. The 5 — 6 slowly growing and almost round whorls have a deep suture; the last or body whorl is somewhat larger and has an indistinct, blunt peripheral ridge. The aperture is mildly oblique, broadly semicircular and somewhat wider than it is high. The straight, sharp margin has a white internal lip. The umbilicus is narrow.

Colouring: the ground colour is chalky white or yellowish white and the shell is either unicoloured or has brown bands. As in other, related species, the banding and patterning is extremely variable.

Size of shell: width 8 — 15 mm, height 5 — 11 mm.

Habitat: forms large populations which live mainly on plants of warm dry sites growing along the coast, but also stretches far inland.

Distribution: the entire European part of the Mediterranean and North Africa.

Family: **Helicidae**

Cernuella neglecta (DRAPARNAUD, 1805), — west Mediterranean. The thick-walled shell closely resembles those of *Helicella itala* and *H. obvia*. It is usually shaped like a compressed sphere, but the spire is much more prominent than in the other two species. It has 5—6 finely and regularly grooved whorls with a shallow suture. The aperture is mildly oval; the margin is sharp and has a distinct internal lip. The umbilicus is much narrower than in *H. itala*. The chief difference compared with the genus *Helicella* is the structure of the reproductive apparatus. *Helicella* species have one dart sac on either side of the vagina, whereas the members of the genus *Cernuella* have two dart sacs together on one side of the vagina.

Colouring: the ground colour is white, but a variable number of relatively wide brown bands runs round the shell right to the end of the body whorl. In some specimens the bands unite to form two or three very wide stripes, so that the shell is almost completely brown. As in all species of the subfamily Helicellinae, pigmentation varies considerably. Sometimes the bands on the upper surface are missing or indistinct, so that the shell, from above, is almost white. The bands fade away on the brownish red or wine-coloured margin (a characteristic feature of this species). Since the margin is also the same colour inside, the high and narrow lip is very conspicuous: it is like porcelain and is usually 1—2 mm from the edge. In some specimens there are two lips very close together. The animal itself is grey or dark-coloured.

Size of shell: together with *Cernuella virgata*, this is one of the most variable species of the genus. Extreme differences are even to be found between adult members of the same population. Width 8.8—20 mm, height 4.2—11.5 mm.

Habitat: grassy slopes, hillsides and rocky localities on a chalky substrate at low and moderately high altitudes. Infiltrates very quickly into secondary habitats — field paths, road and railway embankments and cultivated areas (clover and lucerne fields, cornfields). It is a very expansive species and forms moderately large to very large populations.

Distribution: originally the western part of the Mediterranean (Spain, the south of France, Italy and some Mediterranean islands). From here it has been carried to other European countries – the north of France, Switzerland, Germany, Belgium, Netherlands, Great Britain (probably extinct) the Czech Republic, Slovakia and an isolated population in Poland – either by man (e.g. in exported produce), or by birds (live snails of other species have been found in pigeons' crop: it is not impossible that young specimens can pass through a bird's alimentary tract without being damaged).

Family: Helicidae

1. *Cernuella virgata* (DA COSTA, 1778), **Banded Snail**—Atlantic-Mediterranean. The spherical shell has a tall, bulging spire with 5—7 whorls. The rounded aperture has an internal lip. The umbilicus is narrow and partly concealed by the reflection of the lip. A very variable species; the related *C. neglecta* is more compressed and has a larger umbilicus.
Colouring: the white to rust-coloured shell usually has a dark brown spiral band, which may be thin, broken, composed of spots or missing altogether. The internal lip is white or brown sometimes suffused with pink in the adult.
Size of shell: width 8—25 mm, height 6—19 mm.
Habitat: fairly dry and open chalky sites, dunes, steppes and recent road cuttings on calcareous ground.
Distribution: the entire Mediterranean region and the Atlantic coast of Europe as far as the Netherlands and including the entire coast of the British Isles.

2. *Candidula unifasciata* (POIRET, 1801) — western-central European. The shell, shaped like a compressed sphere, is strong, opaque and finely to coarsely ribbed, especially on the last whorl. In all, it has 4—5 whorls. The aperture is mildly slanting; the margin is sharp and straight and generally has a large, prominent internal lip, which may, however, be flat or even missing. The narrow umbilicus occupies one seventh to one fifth of the width of the shell.
Colouring: white or creamy yellow, with a conspicuous wide band round the periphery. Below this there are usually (but not always) 4—5 narrow bands. The bands are black or brownish and are often broken or blended together.
Size of shell: width 5—9 mm, height 3—6 mm.
Habitat: dry, exposed grassy localities with a chalky substrate. In central Europe it colonizes secondary warm dry microhabitats.
Distribution: the whole of western and central Europe; its eastern limits are the south of Poland, the Czech and Slovak Republics and Hungary. The very similar *C. intersecta* occurs in north-western Europe.

Candidula intersecta (POIRET, 1801). See p. 196.
Candidula gigaxii (PFEIFFER, 1850) (= *Helicella gigaxii*). See p. 196.

3. *Cochlicella barbara* (LINNAEUS, 1758) — Mediterranean. Unlike most other members of the subfamily Helicellinae, this snail has a conically elongate shell. On the upper whorls there is a faint keel, which is gradually lost, so that the last whorl is completely round. In all, there are 7—8 very slightly convex whorls with a shallow suture. The elliptical aperture has a sharp margin; the umbilicus is slit-like.
Colouring: very variable; usually brown bands and reticular or radial streaks on a chalky white or yellowish ground. The related *C. acuta* — often confused with this species — is slimmer (4—7 × 10—20 mm) and has 8—10 whorls.
Size of shell: width 5—8 mm, height 8—12 mm.
Habitat: dry, sunny places with coastal vegetation; often on sand-dunes by the sea.
Distribution: a very common Mediterranean species which has spread along the shores of the Atlantic to the north-western coast of Europe.
Another species, *Cochlicella acuta* (MÜLLER, 1774) occurs on the Atlantic and Channel coasts of the British Isles, Ireland and France.

Family: **Helicidae**

1. *Monacha cartusiana* (MÜLLER, 1774), **Carthusian Snail** — Atlantic-Mediterranean. The spherical, compressed shell has a squatly conical spire; it has thin, but fairly strong, translucent walls, a faintly glossy upper surface and a more polished under side. It is very finely and irregularly sculptured with growth lines. There are 5^1/$_2$—6^1/$_2$ fairly convex whorls; at the aperture the last one is double the width of the penultimate whorl and dominates the others. The aperture slants a little and is elliptical. The sharp and very slightly widened margin contains a low, narrow lip, in the adult like a door-step. The umbilicus is very narrow and is partly hidden by the edge of the columella reflected from the lip.
Colouring: the milky greyish white to yellowish white shell may be tinged brown or pink towards the aperture. The internal lip is whitish brown to pink and shows through the shell as a yellowish white or reddish yellow band bordering the edge of the margin of the aperture.
Size of shell: width 9—17 mm, height 6—10 mm. Its size varies considerably even within the same population and the height of the spire is also variable.
Habitat: meadows and open country in warm lowlands (preferably near flowing water), shrubs and ditches. Occasionally found above 500 m, but never in woods. It will live on dry banks.
Distribution: the entire European part of the Mediterranean, France, the west and south of Switzerland, parts of south-east England, Belgium, the Netherlands, Germany, the Czech Republic and Slovakia. In south-eastern Europe it occurs chiefly in Romania, Hungary, Bulgaria, the southern Ukraine and the Crimea.

2. *Monacha olivieri* (FÉRUSSAC, 1821) — east Mediterranean. The shell is relatively spherical, thin-walled, translucent, faintly glossy, comparatively smooth and irregularly and finely grooved. It is similar in shell form to the previous species. It has two white stripes, the upper one of which runs spirally along the suture to the apex, while the other, which is narrower, leads round the periphery of the shell. The six whorls increase relatively quickly in size; the last one is at first slightly angular, but bulges at the bottom. The aperture is roundly crescent-shaped and its height and width are the same. The margin is straight, with a glossy internal lip. In adult specimens the slit-like umbilicus is completely closed.
Colouring: reddish brown or bluish white, with light, often white stripes, a dark aperture margin in the adult and a lip which is white inside, but appears yellowish red where it shows through the shell.
Size of shell: width 8—20 mm, height 6—13 mm.
Habitat: damp, low-lying country, chiefly beside flowing water, along the coast and in ditches. It also infiltrates into cultivated fields.
Distribution: Sicily, southern Italy, countries of former Yugoslavia, Greece, Turkey and Syria.

Monacha cantiana (MONTAGU, 1803). See p. 197.
Monacha granulata (ALDER, 1830) (= *Ashfordia granulata*). See p. 197.

Family: **Helicidae**

1. *Perforatella bidentata* (GMELIN, 1788) — east European. The shell is spherical, with an elevate conical spire, and its outline is only slightly convex; it is strong, fairly translucent, somewhat irregularly ribbed and dull from above and faintly ribbed and glossy from below. It has 7—8 tightly coiled whorls whose size increases very slowly, and round its circumference it has a distinct, rounded ridge, which becomes indistinct before reaching the aperture. The aperture is angular and mildly obliquely semicircular. The slightly widened, incurved margin has a lip with two large, blunt teeth. The very narrow umbilicus is almost completely hidden by the edge of the columella.

Colouring: light brown with a clearly discernible whitish band round the periphery; the suture is also accompanied by a light-coloured zone; the lip is white to faintly brownish. Albino forms occur in some places.

Size of shell: width 6—10 mm, height 5—7 mm.

Habitat: damp meadow type habitats—valley bottom vegetation, in particular growths of alders and meadows alongside rivers.

Distribution: the entire Carpathian region, the Hungarian lowlands, the northwestern part of the Balkans, the west and centre of the European part of the former USSR, Poland, the Baltic countries. Finland, Sweden, Denmark, Germany, France, Austria, the Czech and Slovak Republics.

2. *Perforatella dibothrion* (KIMAKOWICZ, 1884) — Carpathian. The shell is similar to that of the preceding species, but the spire has a more tumid outline. It is fairly regularly ribbed and dull from above, but more faintly ribbed and glossy from below. It has $6^1/_2$—$7^1/_2$ whorls with a slightly convex upper surface; the last one has a rounded periphery without any discernible angle. The suture, at the aperture, slopes strongly and suddenly downwards. The aperture closely resembles the aperture of *P. bidentata*, but is taller and narrower. The margin is markedly widened, but not curved, and it has a very thick lip. The same teeth are present as in preceding species, but they are very strong and wide, are closer together and obstruct the aperture more than in *P. bidentata*. The parietal callus is almost indistinguishable. The umbilicus is completely (or almost completely) hidden.

Colouring: light brown to reddish brown; the light-coloured peripheral band is wide and very distinct, but the light zone beside the suture is missing. The lip in the aperture is usually brown and it shows plainly through the shell in the form of a yellowish or reddish border.

Size of shell: width 9—12 mm, height 7—10 mm.

Distribution: Romania, the east Carpathians, the Ukraine, the Czech Republic, Slovakia, Poland and Hungary.

Family: **Helicidae**

1. *Perforatella incarnata* (MÜLLER, 1774) (= *Monachoides incarnata*) — central European. The shell is a compressed sphere with a broadly conical spire; it is relatively thin-walled, faintly translucent and dull. The shell surface is regularly and very finely granular (visible with a magnifying glass). It has 6—6^1/$_2$ whorls; on the first third of the last whorl there are signs of an angle at the periphery (young specimens are always angular). The aperture is slanting and somewhat obliquely transversely elliptical. The margin is blunted at the bottom, but otherwise it is sharp and fairly wide; inside it there is a prominent lip like a step, especially at the bottom. The umbilicus is narrow and although it is somewhat hidden by the edge of the columella it is always open. Colouring: the shell is greyish yellow to reddish brown, usually with a light-coloured band round the circumference. The internal lip, which is reddish, appears red or pink where it shows through the shell.
Size of shell: width 12—16 mm, height 9—11 mm.
Habitat: originally a forest species, it inhabits damp rubble and valley vegetation from the lowlands to the mountains; it has also infiltrated into damp cultivated areas in open country.
Distribution: from central France to the west Carpathians.

2. *Perforatella vicina* (ROSSMÄSSLER, 1842) (= *Monachoides vicina*) — Carpathian. The shell closely resembles the shell of *P. incarnata,* but its granular microstructure is distinctly coarser. It has 6—6^1/$_2$ tumid whorls. The margin of the aperture is fairly wide and inside the aperture is an elevated lip. The umbilicus is very narrow and, as distinct from the preceding species, it is completely hidden by the columellar margin. Colouring: the ground colour is yellowish or yellowish white, less often brownish. Inside the aperture the lip is white, but where it shows through the shell it appears yellowish.
Size of shell: width 12—15 mm, height 9—11 mm.
Habitat: chiefly damp valleys with luxuriant vegetation, but also damp mountain forests and bogs.
Distribution: the western Ukraine, Romania, countries of former Yugoslavia, Hungary, Poland, the Czech Republic, Slovakia and an isolated incidence in the Frankish Jura (Germany), south-east of Nuremberg.

3. *Perforatella umbrosa* (C. PFEIFFER, 1828) (= *Urticicola umbrosa*) — east Alpine-Carpathian. The shell is rounded and compressed, with a flatly conical spire; it is relatively thin-walled, fragile, somewhat translucent, faintly glossy, irregularly grooved and finely and somewhat irregularly granular (seen with a magnifying glass). It has 5^1/$_2$ whorls and the periphery of the last one is surmounted by a clearly discernible blunt ridge, which disappears before reaching the aperture. The latter has a pronounced slant and is shaped like a short transverse ellipse. The margin is sharp, is widened throughout, particularly at its base, and it has a very thin internal lip. The extremely wide, funnel-shaped umbilicus accounts for about half the width of the shell. Colouring: light greyish yellow to light reddish brown, with a characteristic pale peripheral band.
Size of shell: width 10—13 mm, height 5.5—7 mm.
Habitat: primarily mountain forests, where it lives in damp valleys, at the foot of rocks and on boggy slopes.
Distribution: Germany, Austria, the Czech Republic, Slovakia, parts of Poland and Hungary, the Ukraine, Romania and countries of former Yugoslavia.

Family: **Helicidae**

1. *Trichia hispida* (LINNAEUS, 1758), **Hairy Snail** — European. The compressed, rounded shell is relatively thin-walled, but fairly strong, slightly translucent and faintly glossy. It is thickly covered with hairs, which measure about 0.3 mm, curve slightly forwards but are sometimes missing from old individuals. The last of the 6—7 whorls has a rounded, more or less distinct peripheral ridge, which fades away at the aperture. The aperture, which is mildly oblique, has the form of a short transverse ellipse; the margin is sharp and slightly widened. The internal lip is elevated and is situated relatively deep in the aperture. The umbilicus is wide to very wide. Like other members of the same genus, *T. hispida* is a very variable species and precisely this variability makes the identification of *Trichia* species very difficult as there are several rather similar snails. Sometimes dissection is necessary to confirm an identification.
Colouring: greyish brown to yellow brown and light reddish brown, with a white inner lip.
Size of shell: width 5—12 mm, height 4—6 mm.
Habitat: varied, includes man-made habitats; absent only in very dry places. Generally in open country.
Distribution: practically the whole of Europe except the most southerly parts.

2. *Trichia striolata* (C. PFEIFFER, 1828), **Strawberry Snail** — north-west European. The shell is larger and has thicker walls than in the preceding species and it is dull; young specimens have small deciduous hairs, adult individuals are always hairless. The last of the six whorls has a clearly discernible, blunt peripheral ridge. The aperture is short and transversely elliptical; the margin is slightly widened and inside it is a flat lip, which, at the base, is raised like a step. The wide umbilicus occupies one eighth to one fifth of the width of the shell.
Colouring: yellowish grey to dark brownish red, usually with a light band round the periphery. Variable.
Size of shell: width 11—14 mm, height 6.5—9 mm.
Habitat: lowland greenwoods, thickets, hedges, ruderal localities and gardens (spread by man).
Distribution: primarily the British Isles, the north-east of France, the Netherlands (the Rhine delta), the southern half of Germany, Austria, the Czech Republic, Slovakia and Hungary.

3. *Trichia lubomirskii* (SLOSARSKI, 1881) — west Carpathian. The shell is sub-globular with a prominent spire and very thin, fragile walls; it is translucent and faintly glossy. Young specimens have short deciduous hairs, adult shells none. There are $4^3/_4$—5 whorls. The slightly slanting aperture is short and transversely elliptical; the margin is sharp and straight. A lip is not usually present and the very narrow umbilicus is partly covered by the widened columellar margin.
Colouring: yellowish white.
Size of shell: width 7—9 mm, height 5.5—7 mm.
Habitat: from the lowlands to high up in the mountains, in dense, damp vegetation, but particularly in nettles.
Distribution: Austria, the Czech and Slovak Republics, the Ukraine and Romania.

Family: Helicidae

1. *Trichia unidentata* (DRAPARNAUD, 1805) — east Alpine-west Carpathian. The shell, with its conical to almost domed spire, is thin-walled but strong, somewhat translucent, dull, finely and irregularly grooved and thickly covered with relatively permanent hairs. The last of its 6—7 convex walls has a faintly indicated, rounded peripheral ridge. The aperture is elongate and transversely elliptical, with a flattened lower edge. The margin is sharp; its columellar and basal segment are somewhat widened and inside is a thick, step-like lip with a wide, blunt tooth, developed to varying extents, which lies roughly in the middle of the basal segment. The umbilicus is very narrow.

Colouring: light brown to reddish brown; the lip is whitish or pink. Albino specimens are occasionally encountered.

Size of shell: width 6—8 mm, height 5—6 mm.

Habitat: a forest species inhabiting damp woods on rubbly ground in valleys in hilly and mountainous country; places with abundant herbaceous vegetation are preferred. Occurs in the Alps at altitudes of up to 2,300 m.

Distribution: Switzerland, Germany, Austria, the Czech Republic, Slovakia and Poland.

2. *Euomphalia strigella* (DRAPARNAUD, 1801) — sub-Pontic. The compressed, spherical shell has a prominent conical spire and relatively thick, strong walls; it is only slightly translucent and faintly glossy and is thickly marked with irregular ribbing and here and there with the remains of longitudinal lines. Young specimens are covered with long hairs, adult shells have none. The six tumid whorls increase regularly in size; from above they are somewhat compressed, but the last one is fully rounded. At the aperture the suture slopes markedly and abruptly downwards. The aperture is distinctly oblique and faintly elliptical, with a slightly indented parietal wall. The margin is sharp; it is somewhat widened at the top, is strikingly widened at the bottom and on the columellar segment, and its edges almost meet on the parietal wall. Inside the margin there is a relatively narrow and only very slightly raised lip. The umbilicus is wide, allows a view of all the whorls and accounts for about one quarter of the width of the shell, but it is partly hidden by the extremely wide columellar margin.

Colouring: light brown to light reddish brown, usually with a pale peripheral band. The lip is whitish or flesh-coloured and shows through the shell as a dark yellow band.

Size of shell: width 12—18 mm, height 9—12 mm.

Habitat: a characteristic species of wooded steppes, it inhabits dry thickets and copses, grassy hillsides and rocky steppes. In cold regions it occurs only in steppes. In the Alps it ascends to 1,760 m.

Distribution: the whole of central and eastern Europe; Austria, the Czech and Slovak Republics, Poland and Hungary, southwards to the north of the Balkans, westwards across the Alps and Germany through Switzerland to the south-east and middle of France and northwards to the south of Scandinavia and Denmark.

Ponentina subvirescens (BELLAMY, 1839) (= *Hygromia revelata*). See p. 198.

Family: **Helicidae**

1. *Helicodonta obvoluta* (MÜLLER, 1774), **Cheese Snail** — sub-Mediterranean. The thick, discoid shell has a flatly sunken central spire. It is relatively thin-walled, but fairly strong, and is mildly translucent when young, dull and irregularly marked with growth lines. Young shells are covered with long (about 0.5 mm) deciduous hairs, which leave plainly visible scars behind them. The 5—6 regularly growing whorls are mildly convex, but are flattened above, below and from the sides. At the aperture the suture continues slowly and smoothly downwards and drops away abruptly only at the very edge. The aperture is oblique and trilobate in adults; the inferior lobe tends to be thinner. The margin is slightly widened and incurved; in the middle of the outer and basal part, the lip is thickened and bluntly elevated. The palatal callus is finely granular and sharply circumscribed, but barely detectable. The umbilicus is deep and wide.
Colouring: dark reddish brown, the lip and teeth white, pink or brown-tinted.
Size of shell: width 11—15 mm, height 5—7 mm.
Habitat: warm sheltered woods on rubbly ground in hills and low mountains; prefers a chalky substrate. In dry weather or in winter hibernation the snail forms a white epiphragm over the aperture.
Distribution: the Pyrenees, Italy, France, southern Belgium, the Netherlands, Germany, Austria, the Czech Republic, Slovakia, Poland and Hungary, the north-western Balkans. Isolated occurrences have also been reported elsewhere in Europe, as in southern England.

2. *Lindholmiola corcyrensis* (FÉRUSSAC, 1839) — Pontic. The shell has a very low and slightly bulging spire with a smooth apex. It is thick-walled and in young specimens it is covered with a quantity of long hairs, which are sometimes preserved on empty shells. There are 6—7 narrow, slowly growing whorls with a clearly discernible continuous peripheral keel; at the aperture the last whorl suddenly sags. The aperture is narrow, crescent-shaped and truncated; the everted margin has a lip. Colouring: light brown, unicoloured or with a trace of a lighter stripe round the periphery. The cinnamon brown lip is often tinged faintly violet.
Size of shell: width 9—12 mm, height 4—6 mm.
Habitat: fallen leaves in lowland and mountain forests.
Distribution: countries of former Yugoslavia, Albania, Greece, Bulgaria, Turkey and isolated incidences in Italy.

1

2

Family: **Helicidae**

Faustina faustina (ROSSMÄSSLER, 1835) (= *Chilostoma faustinum*) — Carpathian. The shell is compressed and rounded (sometimes almost spherical), with a flatly conical spire. It has thick walls, is fairly strong, faintly translucent, glossy and finely and irregularly grooved and has a finely granular larval shell (protoconch) at the apex. The five whorls, which increase regularly and somewhat quickly in size, are slightly convex from above and bulging below and on the sides. The last whorl is completely round; at the aperture the suture at first descends gradually and then abruptly. The aperture has a pronounced slant; it usually has the form of a short ellipse or oval. The margin is relatively wide, with a flat, whitish or brown-tinted lip. The umbilicus is wide and open; it allows a view of all the coils and only a small portion is covered by the reflected columellar margin.

Colouring: basically pale lemon yellow to reddish brown or brownish red. Above the periphery there is generally (though not always) a dark chestnut band. The colouring varies with the climate; in cold conditions at high altitudes yellow populations predominate, while in warmer regions and in the west red-tinted light brown, reddish brown or brownish red forms are the most common. Shells on non-chalky substrates are usually very thin-walled.

Size of shell: width 15—20 mm, height 8—11 mm.

Habitat: damp — and especially shady — rocks, rubble, vegetation, wooded rocky slopes, ruins. It ascends to subalpine level and prefers calcareous rocks, but does not shun other substrates.

Distribution: a large portion of the Carpathian region — Hungary and adjoining areas. Extends northwards into Poland and westwards into the Czech Republic and Slovakia.

Family: **Helicidae**

1. *Faustina trizona rumelica* (ROSSMÄSSLER, 1838) — Balkan. The shell is compressed, rounded, thick-walled, strong and glossy. The upper surface of the 5—6 whorls is relatively flat and they form an only slightly elevated, blunt-tipped spire. The shell is characterized by three bands, the middle one of which is the clearest and darkest and is never absent; the others have a faded appearance and sometimes they almost disappear. The aperture is obliquely oval and sharply truncated. The margin is sharp, very wide, curved and white. The umbilicus, which is about 2.5 mm across, is partly covered by the columellar margin. *Faustina trizona* has several subspecies.
Colouring: straw-coloured with reddish brown stripes, the middle one being the darkest.
Size of shell: width 23—32 mm, height 12—18 mm.
Habitat: in rock fissures, under stones and in fallen leaves in damp, open mixed woods or greenwoods on chalky ground up to 1,500 m.
Distribution: countries of former Yugoslavia, Albania, Bulgaria, Greece, Romania.

2. *Campylaea planospira illyrica* (STABILE, 1864) — south Alpine. The shell is large, compressed and rounded, with a very low, flatly conical spire; it is fairly strong and translucent. The last of the 5—5^1/$_2$ whorls is wide and round. The shell has one pronounced band and growth lines show through it very plainly. The aperture is obliquely elliptical; the margin is short and very wide and is bounded by a narrow white lip. The umbilicus is moderately wide.
Colouring: light brown or greyish brown, often fading to greyish yellow on the under side; the band is reddish brown, the growth zones are yellowish white.
Size of shell: width 26 mm, height 13 mm.
Habitat: a calcicole snail living on or near rocks; it ascends to 1,500 m, but also lives on the floors of valleys.
Distribution: Austria (Carinthia), the Julian Alps and the adjacent parts of former Yugoslavia.

3. *Chilostoma cingulella* (ROSSMÄSSLER, 1837) — an endemic species. The shell is compressed and rounded, faintly translucent and ribbed and the spire is only very slightly raised to an almost even level. At the beginning of the last of the 4^1/$_2$— whorls there is an indistinct trace of a rounded ridge. The aperture is markedly oblique and the margin is widened, with a thin, whitish lip. The umbilicus is wide and open.
Colouring: greyish white, irregularly tinged with brown; just above the periphery there is a brown band.
Size of shell: width 15—18 mm, height 6.5—8 mm.
Habitat: limestone and dolomite rock faces at subalpine and alpine level.
Distribution: endemic to the west Carpathians (Slovakia).

Family: **Helicidae**

1. *Chilostoma cingulata* (STUDER, 1820) — south Alpine. The shell is moderately large, flatly compressed, finely grooved and faintly glossy. It has $5^{1}/_{2}$ slightly convex whorls. The slanting aperture is flesh-coloured inside. The margin is white and everted, with a sham lip and a very wide columellar edge; its edges almost meet. The umbilicus is moderately wide.
Colouring: flesh-tinted grey, with brown transversally arranged spots and a single translucent, chestnut brown peripheral stripe with white edges.
Size of shell: width 20—28 mm, height 10—15 mm.
Habitat: on limestone and dolomite cliffs and rock faces and under stones. Vertical distribution from 600 to 2,000 m.
Distribution: the northernmost part of Italy and the southernmost part of Switzerland. Many subspecies of this very variable species have been described; the two most striking forms are illustrated here. The shell of *Chilostoma cingulata colubrina* (Cr. et Jan) has a brown-speckled surface; it is 28 mm wide and about 13 mm high.

2. *Chilostoma cingulata gobanzi* (FRAUENSFELD, 1867) differs from the typical (nominate) form chiefly in respect of the striking, coarse white ribbing covering the entire surface of the shell. The ribs are curved both above and below and they follow the course of the growth lines from the suture to the umbilicus. Sometimes they fork, or break off in the middle. The ground colour of the shell is bluish white and there is almost always a narrow reddish brown median stripe bordered on either side by a wide and paler stripe; the stripes are all interrupted by the above ribbing. Width of shell 22—27 mm, height 11—14 mm.

3. *Cylindrus obtusus* (DRAPARNAUD, 1805) — an endemic species. The shell is cylindrically elongate and narrows a little towards the bluntly rounded apex; it is strong, opaque, almost smooth and somewhat polished, with 7—8 convex whorls. The aperture is ovally rounded, its height slightly exceeding its width. The margin is sharp and somewhat widened and inside it there is a thin white lip. Despite the completely different form of the elongate shell, the snail's body structure closely resembles that of *Arianta* species.
Colouring: greyish blue, but never purely so (the tip is usually dingy brown).
Size of shell: width 5 mm, height 15 mm.
Habitat: a montane species restricted to chalky substrates, it lives in snow-bound valleys and in depressions and fissures in limestone rocks on damp, grassy slopes in the crooked ('knee') timber zone in the Alps at altitudes of 1,100—2,680 m; it prefers black, humic soil and avoids dry slopes.
Distribution: endemic to the eastern part of the northern limestone Alps (Austria).

Family: **Helicidae**

1. *Dinarica pouzolzi* (DESHAYES, 1830) (= *Campylaea pouzolzi*) — Dinarian. The large, compressed, rounded shell has a flatly conical spire; it is thick-walled, distinctly grooved and faintly glossy. On the shell are three distinct spiral bands — a narrow, sharply defined middle stripe flanked by wider ones, of which the inferior one is particularly wide and fades at its lower edge. The $5^1/_2$—$6^1/_2$ whorls are separated by a relatively deep suture. The aperture is wide and semicircular; the margin is widened, everted and thickened, but without a lip. The very wide umbilicus leaves all the whorls visible.
Colouring: olive green to yellowish brown, with brownish red stripes.
Size of shell: width 24—53 mm, height 17—35 mm. An extremely variable species whose size and colouring depend on the microclimate of the habitat. Individuals from lower, more open localities seem, in general, to be larger than those from mountain forests.
Habitat: limestone regions, from lowlands to mountain forests, up to roughly 1,800 m; commonest in karst valleys on stone walls or in deep rock fissures. Active only at night or during heavy rain.
Distribution: countries of former Yugoslavia and Albania.

2. *Liburnica setosa* (ROSSMÄSSLER, 1836) — Dinarian. The shell is large, compressed, rounded, thin-walled, fragile, densely and finely grooved, dull and covered with relatively long, bristly hairs. It has five whorls with three bands; the two outer bands are generally much paler than the middle one and are sometimes barely visible; the suture is relatively deep. The aperture is sharply truncated and has the form of a short transverse ellipse; the margin is continuous, sharp, wide, everted and labially thickened. The comparatively large umbilicus is overlapped by the beginning of the columellar margin, which generally carries a wide, callus-like tooth.
Colouring: light brownish yellow, with brownish red bands.
Size of shell: width 26—30 mm, height 12—16 mm.
Habitat: as for the preceding species.
Distribution: countries of former Yugoslavia and Albania.

3. *Liburnica denudata* (ROSSMÄSSLER, 1836) — Dinarian. The large, compressed, rounded shell is relatively strong, glossy, smooth, finely grooved and marked with three bands; unlike the preceding species, it is hairless. It has six whorls and a moderately deep suture. The aperture is sharply oblique and rounded; the margin is continuous, prominent and everted and there is a single wide, blunt tooth on the columellar segment. The relatively large umbilicus is partly hidden.
Colouring: yellowish brown, with dark brown stripes running to the uppermost whorls.
Size of shell: width 28—34 mm, height 12—15 mm.
Habitat: as for *Dinarica pouzolzi*.
Distribution: Istria, Dalmatia, Herzegovina and Albania.

Family: Helicidae

1. *Arianta arbustorum* (LINNAEUS, 1758), **Orchard Snail** — central European-sub-Atlantic. The spherical shell has a bluntly conical spire; it is relatively thin-walled but strong, barely translucent, glossy and finely and irregularly grooved and is thickly marked with well developed longitudinal growth lines major ones marking hibernation. The 5—6 convex whorls increase regularly and quickly in size; from above they are slightly flattened, but the body whorl is globular. The aperture is rather oblique and is so shortly elliptical as to be almost rounded. The margin is sharp and widened, with a white, well developed lip. The very narrow umbilicus is almost completely covered over.

Colouring: Variable but mostly chestnut brown, with large numbers of pale yellow spots, particularly underneath, and a dark brown peripheral band. Both the band and the yellow spots are often absent.

Size of shell: width 14—26 mm, height 10—22 mm. Variable in size: populations living high up in the mountains and on an acid ground are much smaller.

Habitat: damp forests of various types up to alpine level (2,700 m); avoids unwooded grassy areas and very dry uplands.

Distribution: the whole of north-western and central Europe; the Czech and Slovak Republics, Poland, Romania, Hungary, the Ukraine, former Yugoslavia and Bulgaria.

2. *Arianta arbustorum alpicola* (FÉRUSSAC, 1821) — alpine. As distinct from the typical form (above), this one has a more clearly grooved and generally lighter coloured shell, so that the dark stripe (if intact) is very conspicuous.

Size of shell: width 16—18 mm, height 12—13 mm.

Habitat: high altitude localities, but also deep valleys, meadows and roadsides. Likewise lives in rocky moraines at the foot of the Alps, indicating that the origination of this small race may have been influenced — *inter alia* — by the glacial periods.

Distribution: throughout the Alps.

3. *Arianta aethiops* (BIELZ, 1867) — Carpathian. The compressed, rounded shell with a mildly elevated spire is thin-walled, fragile and glossy. It is marked with pronounced axial grooves and with faint spiral lines (especially on the last whorl) forming an irregular network. Its five moderately convex whorls grow regularly larger and are separated by a sunken suture. The last whorl is double the width of the penultimate whorl. The aperture is roundly crescent-shaped and oblique and it width almost equals its height. The margin is sharp and widened, with a thin lip showing through the shell as a light yellow border. The narrow umbilicus is partly covered by the widened columellar edge.

Colouring: greenish brown to black, the apex somewhat lighter.

Size of shell: width about 20 mm, height about 12 mm.

Habitat: under stones and in grass in mountain forests (1,400—2,000 m).

Distribution: the east Carpathians (Romania) and the westernmost parts of the former USSR.

Family: **Helicidae**

1. *Helicigona lapicida* (LINNAEUS, 1758), **Lapidary Snail** — sub-Atlantic. The compressed, spherical shell has a narrow, conically bulging spire; it is thick-walled, strong, faintly translucent, dull, indistinctly grooved and relatively coarsely and irregularly granular. The size of the five whorls increases slowly and regularly; their upper surface is flatly compressed and their under side is fully convex, with a sharp peripheral keel. At the aperture, the suture slopes down suddenly and steeply below the keel (shown in the central shell in the illustration opposite). The aperture is markedly oblique and transversely elliptical and its outer edge forms an obtuse angle. The aperture margin is very wide, sharp and continuous, stands away from the parietal wall and has a flat internal lip.

Colouring: greyish brown or light brown, with irregular reddish brown transversal spots.

Size of shell: width 15—17 mm, height 6.6—8.5 mm.

Habitat: lives on various types of rocks (mainly damp) and in forests at the foot of trees (especially beeches). Very abundant on old walls and ruins. Avoids lowlands, grassy plains and regions formed of unconsolidated rocks. Occurs in the Alps at up to 1,700 m.

Distribution: Portugal, the north of Spain, France, the British Isles, Denmark, southern Scandinavia, Germany, the Czech Republic, Slovakia, Austria, the south-west of Poland and the Baltic countries.

2. *Drobacia banatica* (ROSSMÄSSLER, 1838) — Carpathian. The shell is large, widely lenticular and thick-walled, with a squatly conical or conically convex spire; its upper and middle whorls have a densely granular surface, while on the lower whorls there are fine spiral lines, so that the surface as a whole is matt. The $5^{1}/_{2}$—6 faintly convex whorls have a peripheral keel; the body whorl, opposite the aperture, is bluntly keeled and sags a little way below the edge. Its aperture is transversely oval and truncated and its edges are very far apart. The margin is sharp and wide, with a white lip. About one third of the moderately wide umbilicus is covered by the columellar edge.

Colouring: the shell is light to dark brown or olive brown, with a narrow brownish red stripe just above the peripheral line.

Size of shell: width 24—30 mm, height 16—18 mm; the aperture is 17 mm wide and 13 mm high.

Habitat: in forests under stones and rotting wood (stumps, timber), on plants and generally in damp places.

Distribution: Romania (Transylvania, the Banat region) and adjoining territories. In the last interglacial period the area of this species stretched much further westwards, across Austria, the Czech and Slovak Republics to Germany.

Family: **Helicidae**

1. *Isognomostoma isognomostoma* (SCHRÖTER, 1784) — central European. The compressed spherical shell, with its squatly bulging spire, is thin-walled, not very strong, mildly translucent, dull, very finely and irregularly grooved and coarsely granular, with longish (0.6 m), slightly curved hairs, some of which rub off in the adult. The 5—6 convex, rounded whorls expand slowly and regularly. The moderately deep suture drops away somewhat abruptly over a short distance at the aperture. The oblique aperture forms a triangle whose base is the arching parietal wall. The margin is very wide (but not everted) and sharp; its outer and basal segment have a slightly elevated strip-like lip and in the middle of each segment is a large, blunt tooth. The aperture thus has three teeth, which take up a lot of space, leaving only a small area for the snail. The narrow umbilicus is completely — or almost completely — covered by the columellar margin.
Colouring: light reddish brown.
Size of shell: width 7—11 mm, height 4—7 mm.
Habitat: forests on a rubble substrate in hilly country and mountains, from 300 to 1,700 m. It lives mostly among stones and under fallen trees and rotting wood and avoids lowlands and unwooded grassy plateaus.
Distribution: central and eastern Europe, the Alps (especially their northern part), mountains in Germany, the Czech Republic, Slovakia, Poland, Hungary, the Ukraine and Romania.

2. *Isognomostoma holosericum* (STUDER, 1820) (= *Causa holosericum*) — Alpine. The shell is thick and discoid, with a level or only slightly prominent spire; it is thin-walled, fairly strong, mildly translucent, matt, very faintly and irregularly grooved and very finely and densely granular. It is thickly covered with very short, hooked hairs arranged in regular rows. The $4^1/_2$—5 whorls expand slowly and regularly; their upper surface is slightly, and their under side markedly, convex and there are signs of a rounded ridge on the peripheral line, situated very high up. The suture at first descends very smoothly and slowly, but at the aperture, over a short distance, it falls away abruptly. The aperture is relatively oblique and roughly square, with rounded corners. The margin is very wide and sharp, with a large and bluntly elevated lip which forms one large tooth on the outer and basal segment each; in addition to the lower tooth there is usually another tooth-like protuberance in the direction of the columella. The umbilicus is wide and open.
Colouring: light reddish brown; the lip is white, tinged with brown.
Size of shell: width 9—12 mm, height 5—6 mm.
Habitat: chiefly coarse rubble in upland and mountain forests and often in conifer woods on acid rock substrates, usually from 800 to 2,000 metres.
Distribution: the Alps, the Swiss Jura and the Czech and Slovak Republics; occasionally in Germany.

Family: Helicidae

1. *Murella muralis* (MÜLLER, 1774) — west Mediterranean. The shell has a domed and sometimes only very slightly elevated spire. Its upper surface is finely grooved, with a quantity of streaks or zigzag spots forming three broken bands. On its under surface there is always a fourth stripe — sometimes not very distinct — formed of irregularly shaped spots. There are five whorls with a flat suture. The aperture is wide, crescent-shaped and slanting; the everted margin has a clearly discernible lip. In adult specimens the umbilicus is completely closed.
Colouring: greyish white with brown or grey spots; the parietal wall of the aperture is always dark brown. Near the columellar margin is a small brown spot on the white lip.
Size of shell: width 19—20 mm, height 9—10 mm.
Habitat: limestone rocks and old walls.
Distribution: Italy and the neighbouring islands, the south of France, the Balearic Islands and Spain.

2. *Marmorana serpentina* (FÉRUSSAC, 1801) — Apennine. The shell is a compressed sphere with a slightly elevated spire, sometimes a blunt-edged keel and thick walls. It has 4—5 whorls with a fine median suture. The aperture is wide and crescent-shaped; the aperture margin is somewhat widened and has a clearly discernible white lip. The umbilicus is generaly occluded in the adult.
Colouring: chalky white or dingy yellow, with rows of brown drop-shaped or zig-zag, irregular spots forming five bands. At the base of the columellar margin of the aperture there is always a brown umbilical spot which sometimes covers the entire columellar edge and the wall of the aperture.
Size of shell: width 19—21 mm, height 9.5—10.5 mm.
Habitat: lives mainly on the walls of houses and ruins.
Distribution: Italy, Sardinia and Corsica.

3. *Theba pisana* (MÜLLER, 1774), **Sandhill Snail** — Mediterranean. The shell is a slightly compressed sphere with $5^1/2$—6 mildly convex whorls and a shallow suture. Young specimens have a sharp peripheral keel, but in adults the periphery is only very faintly ridged. The elliptical aperture has an internal lip and a sharp margin. The narrow umbilicus is partly covered by the everted columellar edge.
Colouring: variable, white, yellowish red, occasionally pink; the growth lines are crossed by fine spiral grooving, usually with differently patterned spiral bands, which are often faint, translucent, broken or joined together. Pale pink inside the lip of adults. Protoconch of apex usually dark.
Size of shell: width 12—25 mm, height 9—20 mm.
Habitat: dry localities, usually near the sea; especially dunes, where the snails can be found clinging to plants.
Distribution: the whole Mediterranean region, various places along the European shores of the Atlantic including Channel Islands, parts of southwestern Britain, France, Belgium and the Netherlands. Isolated incidences elsewhere in Europe.

Family: **Helicidae**

1. *Otala lactea* (MÜLLER, 1774) — west Mediterranean. The shell is large, compressed and rounded (occasionally with an elevated spire), thick-walled and almost smooth. The typical form has four wide, sharply defined bands, which are usually crossed by irregular, milky white markings. It has five slightly convex whorls, which first increase slowly and then very quickly in size; the body whorl widens at the aperture. The aperture is very oblique and transversely elongate; the margin is blunt throughout, somewhat thickened and only mildly everted. The columellar edge is long and thickened, with a wide, obtuse-angled corner. The umbilicus is completely closed.
Colouring: greyish yellow, very rarely almost chalky white, with brown bands. The parietal wall and the inside of the aperture, the margin and the columellar edge are dark brown. The colouring is sharply defined, but is extremely variable, ranging from pure white specimens, via the most diverse degrees of interruption of the bands, to unicoloured chestnut brown. *O. lactea* is often confused with the similar *O. punctata* (France).
Size of shell: width 20—40 mm, height 13—23 mm.
Habitat: limestone rocks, the walls of Moorish castles, occasionally on *Opuntia* (prickly-pear) plants; in flat country the snail hides among the blades and leaves of densely growing plants, or in thorny pod-bearing bushes. In Spain it used to be called 'caracol del trueno', i. e. thunder or storm snail, and people believed that it would protect their house against being struck by lightning.
Distribution: the south of Spain, Portugal, the Balearic Islands, Morocco, Algeria.

2. *Eobania vermiculata* (MÜLLER, 1774) — circum-Mediterranean. The shell is a compressed sphere with thick walls, regular accretion lines and a finely reticulated surface. It has five variable dark stripes, which are often joined together or broken. The last of the five mildly convex whorls — which have a shallow suture — slopes abruptly downwards at the aperture. The aperture is flattened and noticeably oblique. The wide margin usually has a thick white lip. The umbilicus is completely closed.
Colouring: very variable, but mostly creamy white or yellowish red covered with a whitish reticular pattern; the stripes are brownish red or dark brown.
Size of shell: width 22—30 mm, height 14—27 mm.
Habitat: originally inhabited steppes, but has secondarily colonized fields, thickets, gardens, vineyards and roadsides.
Distribution: a common species in all the Mediterranean countries and islands Asia Minor and the Crimea. Also occurs in isolated localities in other countries.

Family: **Helicidae**

1. *Iberus gualterianus* (LINNAEUS, 1758) — an endemic species. The large, compressed shell differs markedly from that of all the other members of the family illustrated. Its upper surface is quite flat, its under side bulges and it has a sharp, compressed keel and thick walls. Its entire surface is criss-crossed with furrows and is therefore unevenly tuberculate. The five whorls overlap each other and above the keel they are straight or mildly concave. The aperture is markedly oblique and is shaped like an axe-head. The margin is everted, simple and grooved. The umbilicus is usually completely covered by the widened white columellar margin.
Colouring: light coffee brown with white lip; the animal is greyish yellow.
Size of shell: width 34—40 mm, height 17—20 mm.
Habitat: bare limestone rocks; during the daytime the snail hides in shaded crevices in the rocks.
Distribution: the south of Spain, where it occurs in a number of forms whose shells range from completely round to sharply keeled.

2. *Iberus marmoratus* (FÉRUSSAC, 1801) — an endemic species. The shell, which has no umbilicus, is a compressed, finely grooved, fairly thin and glossy sphere marked with 4—5 bands formed of connected arrow-shaped spots. A difference in the pattern makes the upper surface of the whorls, between the third band and the apex, much darker than the under side. There are five fairly convex whorls; the penultimate one still grows regularly, but the last one is larger and rounded, with a more bulging under side, and it dips almost regularly deeper in front. The aperture is roundly crescent-shaped. The margin is sharp, with a slightly slanting upper edge; its upper and outer edge are markedly everted and it is lined with a thin, lustrous lip.
Colouring: whitish or yellowish with brown bands; the pattern on the upper surface is brown or grey.
Size of shell: width 17—22 mm, height 9.5—11.5 mm.
Habitat: limestone rocks.
Distribution: the south of Spain.

3. *Iberus alonensis* (FÉRUSSAC, 1801) — an endemic species. The large, distinctly widened shell is thick-walled, strong and only slightly glossy. The five quickly expanding whorls form a bluntly convex spire. The suture is mildly sunken. The aperture is obliquely and semicircularly rounded. The margin is only widened or slightly everted, with a thin white lip. The umbilicus is generally completely hidden in the adult.
Colouring: whitish or greyish, with five light brown stripes; the three on the upper surface are very close together, while the two on the under side are further apart and generally have a border whiter than the ground colour. The stripes are often absent and in that case the shell is plain-coloured or speckled.
Size of shell: width 30—38 mm, height 16—19 mm.
Habitat: limestone rocks.
Distribution: the south of Spain.

Family: **Helicidae**

Cepaea nemoralis (LINNAEUS, 1758), **Brown-lipped** or **Grove Snail** — west European. The shell is a compressed sphere with a conical spire with almost straight (only faintly convex) contours; it is relatively thin-walled, strong, slightly translucent, glossy, faintly and irregularly grooved and very finely granular. It has $4^1/_2 - 5^1/_2$ slightly convex whorls, whose size increases fairly quickly and regularly; at the aperture, the suture slopes abruptly downwards over a fairly long distance. The aperture has the form of a very short, oblique ellipse. The edge of the thickened aperture margin is coloured both inside and outside (a typical character of this species); the linear and oblique part of the lower segment of the margin is relatively longer, less flatly elevated and strikingly straight, while its curving edge almost touches the wall of the shell over a long segment stretching from the columella to the lowest point of the margin.

Colouring: extremely variable: yellow, pink or reddish shades of ground colour, with diversely combined and usually dark brown bands, of which the fifth or the fourth is the widest. The bands often fuse in the 5-banded forms. Unbanded and one-banded forms are common. The aperture margin has a deep black-brown edge, both inside and outside, and the umbilical area is the same colour. The lip is usually reddish brown, while the very thin parietal callus is dark reddish brown and is outwardly sharply circumscribed. The brown lip usually distinguishes this snail from *C. hortensis*, but white-lipped varieties of *C. nemoralis* sometimes occur. Further inside the shell, the dark colouring gradually fades away. Together with the next species, this is one of the most variable snails as regards colouring and markings. The outer layer of shell (periostracum) gives the surface a varnished look — it becomes matt when the periostracum is worn away.

Size of shell: width 18—25 mm, height 12—22 mm, occasionally larger.

Habitat: forests, thickets, sloping surfaces, steppes and dunes. Occurs in the Alps up to 1,400 m, in the Pyrenees up to 1,800 m. In some countries lives only in orchards, gardens and parks near human habitations.

Distribution: very widespread throughout western Europe, in Scandinavia it lives only along the coast; it inhabits the Baltic coast as far as Lithuania and Latvia and in central Europe it occurs in the western part of Hungary, Germany and northern Bohemia. In the Balkan peninsula it is to be found as far as Bosnia. It has also been carried to many other places outside its main distribution area.

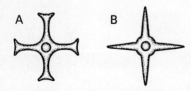

Cross section of love dart of *C. hortensis* (A) and *C. nemoralis* (B). This feature of anatomy serves to distinguish the two species and is useful in populations which have abnormal lip colour.

Family: **Helicidae**

1. *Cepaea hortensis* (MÜLLER, 1774), **White-lipped** or **Garden Snail** — west-central European. The shell closely resembles that of the preceding species but is smaller, with a neater mouth and usually a white lip. It is a compressed sphere and its conical spire has very slightly, but discernibly convex contours. The 5—$5^1/_2$ mildly convex whorls expand fairly quickly and regularly in size. On the edge of the widened margin there is a white lip which, from the outside, appears light yellow; the parietal callus is very thin, light-coloured and sharply demarcated. Occasional specimens occur which have a brown lip, but they can be identified on dissection of the dart sac (see page 162).

Colouring: the ground colour is yellow or pink. The brown bands are very variable; there may be only one, or five which can fuse and unbanded forms are also common. The fourth band below the periphery is generally the widest.

Size of shell: somewhat variable; average width 14—21 mm, average height 10—17 mm.

Habitat: forests, hedges along sunken lanes, shrubs on road-cuttings, steppes and dunes, but generally damper and colder localities than for *C. nemoralis*, although the two often occur together. Ascends the Alps to 2,000 m. Likewise frequents gardens, orchards and old walls.

Distribution: the whole of western Europe, the British Isles, southern Scandinavia, the Alps, central Europe, the Baltic countries, the Czech Republic, Slovakia and Hungary.

2. *Cepaea hortensis* f. *fuscolabiata* KREGLINGER, 1870. Unlike the preceding typical form, this one has a unicoloured red (rarely yellow) shell; the edge of the margin is more or less dark brown and the lip shows yellow through the shell. This form has a scattered incidence of single individuals and whole populations; it often occurs together with the normally striped form.

3. *Cepaea silvatica* (DRAPARNAUD, 1801) — west Alpine. The shell is a compressed sphere with a conical spire, very fine grooving and regular, indistinct spiral lines. Of the five typical bands, the three lower ones are generally bold, while the first two are almost always broken up into spots. The 5—6 regularly expanding whorls are clearly convex and the last one slopes abruptly downwards in front of the aperture, which is markedly oblique and elliptical. The thin, sharp margin has a white lip and an everted columellar edge with a fine, sharp, white callus and a brown spot. The umbilicus is completely covered over.

Colouring: yellowish or whitish with brownish red stripes.

Size of shell: width 18—25 mm, height 12—16 mm.

Habitat: mountain forests and meadows at altitudes of 500 to 2,400 m.

Distribution: the western Alps — the south of France, northern Italy, Switzerland and Germany.

Family: **Helicidae**

1. *Cepaea vindobonensis* (FÉRUSSAC, 1821) — south-east European. The shell is a compressed sphere with thick, strong, opaque, faintly glossy walls with distinctive axial grooves distinguishing this species from others in the genus. It has $5—5^1/2$ fully convex whorls whose size increases fairly quickly. The aperture is markedly oblique and is produced slightly sideways at its base. The margin is widened and has an internal lip.

Colouring: the ground colour is whitish, cream or greyish yellow and is always striped. The first and second bands are usually narrow and light brown (the second is often missing or only faintly indicated); the third, fourth and fifth are generally wider and dark brown to blackish brown (the fifth is the widest of all and is situated very close to the umbilical region).

Size of shell: width 20—25 mm, height 17—21 mm.

Habitat: grassy slopes, rocks, thickets and wooded steppe formations. It also frequently occurs in secondary habitats (vineyards, quarries, embankments, etc) and high up in the mountains on south-facing limestone slopes (in the Alps up to 1,500 m).

Distribution: Romania, Hungary, the Czech Republic, Slovakia, Poland, the southern parts of the former USSR to the Caspian Sea, the Balkans, Austria, the north of Italy, Germany.

2. *Macularia niciensis* (FÉRUSSAC, 1822) — an endemic species. The shell is a compressed sphere with a flatly conical spire; it is strong, slightly translucent and finely grooved and has five broken bands, the middle one of which is the widest. The five fairly convex whorls expand regularly, the last or body whorl is rounded and drops suddenly and deeply away in front. The aperture has a strong slant and a broadly oval crescent-shaped form. The margin is not everted, but is rather wide and has a lip. The columellar edge is straight, with a thick, compressed callus, The umbilicus is either absent, or is very narrow and covered by the columellar margin.

Colouring: chalky white or dingy greyish white with square brown spots arranged in stripes; the lip and the parietal wall are mauvish.

Size of shell: width 20—25 mm, height 11—14 mm.

Habitat: rocks and old walls.

Distribution: endemic to the Maritime Alps (the south of France and northern Italy).

3. *Condrigtonia condrigtonia* (GRAY, 1834) — southern Balkan. The shell is generally a compressed sphere with six slightly domed, irregularly grooved whorls. Of its five stripes, the two lower ones are usually constant and distinctly coloured, while the three upper ones are broken and are formed of rows of spots. The aperture is very oblique and is wider than it is high. The almost straight margin is usually lined with a thin white lip.

Colouring: greyish white, yellowish or brownish, with brown or black stripes.

Size of shell: width 40 — 50 mm, height 30 —50 mm.

Habitat: rock fissures.

Distribution: Greece and the Greek islands.

Family: **Helicidae**

1. *Helix aspersa* (MÜLLER, 1774), **The Common Garden Snail** — Atlantic-Mediterranean. The shell is spherical, with a short, conical, blunt spire; it is irregularly marked with growth lines, and is typically sculptured with folds. There are typically five dark broken spiral bands on the shell giving it a blotched appearance; the second and third generally run together and sometimes all three upper bands coalesce. The shell consists of $4^1/_2$—5 moderately convex, relatively quickly expanding whorls. The body whorl is very large and globular and curves steeply downwards at the aperture. The aperture is truncated and drawn out sideways; it is roundly oval and mildly cut away at the top. The white-lipped margin is markedly widened all the way round from the columella to the top corner; its outer edge is everted and the columellar edge is relatively extended; the edges are joined together by a thin white parietal callus. The umbilicus is completely covered by the columellar edge.
Colouring: usually light brown, sometimes yellow with brown stripes, often white and spotted. The colouring and markings are very variable.
Size of shell: width 25—40 mm, height 25—35 mm.
Habitat: forests, thickets, fields, rocks, seaside dunes; also parks, vineyards and gardens, where it is frequently a pest.
Distribution: the entire Mediterranean region, the oceanic part of western Europe, here and there in the central part of western Europe, North Africa, Asia Minor. It has also become a synanthropic species in the north of Great Britain and in Belgium, Netherlands, the west of Switzerland and Germany. It has been introduced to various countries and continents all over the world. Like other large species it is edible.

1. *Helix aperta* BORN, 1778 — west Mediterranean. The shell is an obliquely oval bulging, irregularly grooved, thin-walled, translucent and fairly glossy sphere with only $3^1/_2$—4 whorls. The first two whorls are very small, the penultimate is convex and the dominant body whorl, which is large and globular, curves down slowly and regularly in front, making the bluntly conical spire insignificant. The aperture is slightly oblique and very large (it accounts for almost four fifths of the height of the shell), vertical, oval and cut away over a short distance, but deeply, at the top. The blunt, white-lipped margin is joined together by a thin white callus. The umbilicus is completely hidden.
Colouring: a uniform yellowish brown, sometimes marked with a network or row of speckles. The animal is light greenish brown.
Size of shell: width 20—26 mm, height 24—30 mm.
Habitat: it chiefly inhabits vineyards, where it spends most of the year buried in the ground. It emerges at the end of the summer and the beginning of the autumn and lives on grass and vine leaves.
Distribution: southern Europe, North Africa. It is edible and has delicate and very tasty flesh.

Family: **Helicidae**

Helix pomatia LINNAEUS, 1758, **Roman** or **Edible Snail** — central European — south-east European. The spherical shell has a conical, prominent spire; it is large, thick-walled, very strong, opaque, faintly glossy and finely and irregularly bluntly sculptured with thin, uneven, axial lines. It has $4^1/_2$—5 highly convex whorls whose size increases quickly and regularly, so that the last one dominates the rest. On the last quarter of the body whorl the suture descends smoothly and gently to the aperture. The aperture is oblique, very roomy, approximately round or very broadly oval, with a sharp upper corner, and is higher than it is wide. The margin is slightly widened, blunt and lined with a flat, whitish or brownish lip. The narrow umbilicus is hidden by the thickened columellar edge to such an extent that only the umbilical slit is left; it is rare for the umbilicus to be covered over completely. Sinistral or scalariform individuals are occasionally found. In old specimens the periostracum is usually worn away.

Colouring: whitish grey to light yellowish brown, often with faintly mauve to dark violet bands. The first band, which is narrow, lies just below the suture; the second and third generally run together. The bands are not always clearly defined and completely irregular darker cross stripes frequently appear.

Size of shell: width 32—50 mm, height 30—50 mm. This and *H. lucorum* are the largest species of land snails in Europe.

Habitat: light copses and thickets, mainly in warm, low-lying country. The snail also often appears on cultivated ground. It prefers a chalky substrate and in suitable places it ascends to higher altitudes (in the Alps up to 2,000 m). In cold forested regions on acid soil — where it is likewise to be found — it is mostly a secondary inhabitant, brought there artificially.

In some countries the Roman Snail is regarded as a great delicacy. Since the local supply is insufficient to meet the demand, the snails are bred artificially and are often exported. The best time for transporting them is the winter, when they temporarily form a calcareous epiphragm, but they taste the best in the spring, when their calcium salts content is the lowest. When the snails are cooked, these salts are precipitated and give the flesh of autumn specimens an unwanted side flavour. Some countries have resolved seasonal transport problems by exporting the snails tinned.

Distribution: southern part of the British Isles, Germany, Denmark, the Netherlands, south of Sweden, Belgium, the east of France, the Alps, northern Italy, former Yugoslavia, Bulgaria, Romania, Hungary, the Czech Republic, Slovakia, Poland and the Ukraine.

Helix pomatia seems to have been popular with the Romans and its English vernacular name indicates that they intentionally introduced it into Britain, where it is unknown as a fossil in pre-Roman deposits. Writers like Varro and Pliny mention the special vessels in which these snails were kept. In Roman ruins in different parts of Europe (e. g. Rheinbach and Lake Constance), the kitchen waste, alongside bones, was found to include a large number of shells of the species *Helix pomatia* and evidently of *Helix aspersa* as well.

Family: **Helicidae**

1. *Helix lucorum* LINNAEUS, 1758 — Pontic-Mediterranean. The shell is spherical, slightly compressed and globular, with a large rounded apex; the upper whorls are slightly grooved, with distinct spiral lines, while the body whorl is more strongly sculptured by axial growth lines. The shell is thick-walled, relatively smooth and mildly translucent. The markings are very irregular; the second band usually blends with the third and the fourth with the fifth, but sometimes only the second with the third; it is rare to find all five stripes. The five whorls are separated by a deep suture. The aperture is wide and oval and almost as broad as it is high. The margin is slightly thickened, blunt and somewhat widened. The columellar edge is drawn out and everted, so that it covers the umbilicus as a blackish brown lamella. The umbilicus is very small, but is seldom completely closed.

Colouring: very variable; the ground colour is white, but apart from a white median stripe, which is rarely absent, it is almost always super-imposed with wide reddish brown, blotched bands. At irregular intervals, blackish brown growth lines cross the bands — these are points where growth stopped for hibernation or aestivation. The margin is dark brown, the parietal wall gunmetal grey and the ends of the bands blackish brown. Although a similar shell to *H. pomatia,* this species has a more colourful and patterned shell.

Size of shell: very variable; width 35—55 mm, height 20—50 mm.

Habitat: diverse dry and damp localities, slopes overgrown with vegetation, thickets, parks, gardens, open woods; in mountains it ascends to 1,200 m.

Distribution: Italy, countries of former Yugoslavia, Bulgaria, Romania, the Crimea and the Caucasus and Asia Minor.

2. *Helix melanostoma* DRAPARNAUD, 1801 — west Mediterranean. The shell is swollen and spherical, with a short, conical spire and a rather small apex. It is axially grooved (chiefly the upper half, but sometimes equally strongly throughout) and has four whorls. The body whorl expands markedly and dominates the rest; the suture is not very deep. The aperture is pointedly oval and its height is somewhat greater than its width. The margin is a little thickened, blunt and lined with a flat, slightly elevated lip. The umbilicus is completely hidden.

Colouring: the ground colour is reddish grey; the upper half is darker and generally marked with three very light, indistinct bands, which are generally pronounced only on the middle whorls. The parietal wall is light brownish violet; the lip and the inner wall of the aperture are dark brown.

Size of shell: width 25—40 mm, height 25—50 mm.

Habitat: vineyards, olive groves, gardens. Appears in small numbers after heavy rain. Edible.

Distribution: the south of France, Spain, the west Mediterranean islands, Algeria and Tunisia.

Class: **Bivalvia** — **Bivalves**
Order: **Eulamellibranchia**

Family: **Margaritiferidae** — **Freshwater Pearl Mussels**
The shells have two identical, mostly flattened and thick-walled valves with shallow umbonal cavities. The conchiolin layer is dull and black. Pearl mussels live in clean flowing water in the northern hemisphere and they have been adversely affected by changes in the environment. Pearl fishing once provided a livelihood for many families.

Margaritifera margaritifera (LINNAEUS, 1758), **Freshwater Pearl Mussel** — Holarctic. The valves are very thick-walled, heavy and kidney-shaped. The umbones are relatively flat and are usually severely corroded. The lower ventral edge of the valve is always distinctly concave in the middle. The valves are asymmetrical, with the posterior part 2.5 to 3 times longer than the anterior part. The hinge: the right cardinal tooth is broadly and bluntly conical and so are the two left teeth. The thick hinge plate, which widens posteriorly, has no lateral teeth. The inner surface of the valves are mother-of-pearl.
Colouring: the periostracum of young specimens is dark brown; in later life it is nearly black and almost dull and is thickly marked with irregular growth lines.
Size: length 95—140 mm, height 50—60 mm, breadth 30—40 mm. The concentric lines on the surface of the valves, conspicuous for their different colours, show where growth of the shell was interrupted in the winter. They are also known as annual rings, but they are not an absolutely reliable criterion of age, since a protracted deficient food supply can also lead to the formation of secondary lines during the growth period. Counting the annual rings can be used satisfactorily only from the age of 15 years upwards. In very old pearl mussels, on the other hand, it is difficult to differentiate the individual growth lines. The best way to determine age is to count the growth lines on the ligament. From the width of the increments it would seem that the main mass of a pearl mussel's shell is formed between the ages of 30 and 40 years; at 50 years growth slows down and at 60 years it virtually stops. The oldest specimens found were about 90 years old.
The popularity of pearl mussels is due primarily to their ability to produce pearls; these are formed the most frequently at the edge of the mantle. If cells from the surface of the mantle penetrate inside it, they form a pearl sac in which, in time, a pearl is secreted. A foreign body which enters the shell as a result of injury, for instance, and penetrates the mantle together with the surface cells, can also end up as the core of a pearl, but it is not essential to the pearl-forming process.
Habitat: cold, clean streams and small rivers in regions with non-calcareous bedrock and soft water (primary rocks). Today the Pearl Mussel is disappearing, even in regions in which it was once abundant. Its disappearance is due to pollution of the water by industrial waste and to the increased use of chemicals in agriculture, which drain into the river systems.

Distribution: the Czech and Slovak Republics, Germany, Scandinavia, the British Isles, the northernmost European part of the former USSR. Western and southern Europe are inhabited by the related *M. auricularia*, which will occur in harder water.

Family: **Unionidae** — **Freshwater Mussels**

The shell, which has identical valves, is pearly, with a thin layer of conchiolin and usually with a sculptured umbo, a residue of the larval shell. The inside of the valves is lined with mother-of-pearl. The umbonal cavities are deep. In most species the hinge has two cardinal and two lateral teeth in the left valve and one cardinal and one lateral tooth in the right valve. The family is represented on all the continents.

1. *Unio pictorum* (LINNAEUS, 1758), **Painter's Mussel** — European. The valves are moderately thick-walled, elongate, narrow and pointedly tongue-shaped, swollen in front and in the middle and cuneiformly tapering at the back. Their length is more than twice their height. The valves are asymmetrical: on the anterior part, which lies well to the front, the lunule forms a rounded angle; the slightly elevated escutcheon forms a very blunt, rounded angle. The posterior part of the valve is about three times longer than the anterior part. The hinge: the cardinal teeth are relatively large. The right one is wedge-like, blunt, roughly notched and triangular or trapezoid in form. The left teeth are both long, low, flat and sharp; the anterior one in particular has a finely notched edge, while the posterior one, which is pressed to it from inside, is shorter and often stunted.
Colouring: the periostracum is mostly olive or brownish yellow, with narrow, dark accretion bands, but no rays.
Size: length 60—140 mm, height 25—60 mm, breadth 23—31 mm.
Habitat: rivers, pools, reservoirs, large brooks, mill streams and fishponds in low-lying country; it prefers quiet water.
Distribution: it forms several subspecies in Europe (except the southernmost parts); in the east it still occurs in the Ural basin and the Caucasus.

2. *Unio tumidus* RETZIUS, 1788, **Swollen River Mussel** — European. The valves are very thick-walled, slightly elongate and pointedly oval; anteriorly they bulge and their length is roughly double their height. The umbones are swollen, are situated a fairly long way anteriorly and are sculptured with folds. The anterior end is wide, arched and tumid. The lunule is absent or indistinct; the escutcheon is barely discernible and is very blunt. The posterior end of the shell forms an almost symmetrical, rounded point and is $2^1/_2$ to $2^3/_4$ times longer than the anterior part. The hinge: the cardinal teeth are cuneiform; the right one is irregularly tricuspid and is roughly notched; the two left ones are separated by a deep furrow. The posterior part of the hinge plate, with the lateral teeth, is only slightly inclined. The species of *Unio* are distinguished by the shape and tumidity of the shell.
Colouring: the periostracum is yellowish brown and is generally marked with dark bands and green rays.
Size: length 65—80 mm, height 30—45 mm, breadth 24—30 mm.
Habitat: rivers, creeks, fishponds and lakes in low-lying country.
Distribution: most of Europe except the Mediterranean region and high altitudes in central Europe; eastwards as far as the Ural and Transcaucasia. A fairly constant species with only two subspecies.

1

2

Family: **Unionidae — Freshwater Mussels**

1. *Unio crassus* RETZIUS, 1788 — European. The valves are elliptical or oval and shorter than in the preceding species, so that their height is usually more than half their length. The umbones are faintly prominent and unless they are corroded they are densely marked with concentric puckered folds. The anterior end is bluntly rounded and minus a lunule, while the posterior end is usually broadly tongue-shaped. The lower edge is either straight or slightly concave in the middle and seldom convex. The escutcheon is faintly indicated and the posterior edge leads away from it in a protracted curve. The hinge: the cardinal tooth of the right valve is bluntly and cuneiformly conical, with a furrowed outer surface and an irregularly notched crest. The two main teeth of the left valve are bluntly pyramidal; they lie one behind the other and are separated by a deep oblique furrow. In front of the lateral teeth the hinge plate is slightly bent.
Colouring: the periostracum is predominantly dark brown (less often light brown) and is occasionally marked with green rays.
Size: length 50—70 mm, height 23—33 mm, breadth 25—35 mm.
Habitat: large streams and rivers with a sandy to muddy bed. As distinct from the preceding species, this one requires running water.
Distribution: occurs in several races in most European countries.

2. *Microcondylaea compressa* (MENKE, 1828) — south European. The shell has the form of a short or longish ellipse; it is compressed, thin-walled and relatively fragile and the valves are asymmetrical. The umbone is low and finely sculptured with folds which run almost parallel to the growth lines and sometimes form double waves. The posterior end of the shell is somewhat two-angled; the anterior end is narrow and its upper edge is sometimes mildly curved. The surface of the shell is marked with irregular concentric grooves, but is almost smooth. On either valve there is a single low, mildly rounded, nodular tooth, which is often completely reduced. Lateral teeth are present only as traces.
Colouring: the colouring of the periostracum is variable and ranges from almost black to light green; the nacreous layer is bluish white and relatively dull.
Size: like the shape, size varies with the locality. Length 50—70 mm, height 28—34 mm, breadth 13—20 mm.
Habitat: clean rivers and lakes.
Distribution: this is not known exactly, but the species occurs mainly in the north of Italy, parts of former Yugoslavia, Bulgaria and Albania.

1

2

Family: **Unionidae — Freshwater Mussels**

1. *Anodonta cygnea* (LINNAEUS, 1758), **Swan Mussel** — Eurosiberian. The shell is elongate, ovoid and thin-walled. The low, oval eschutcheon is almost level with the umbones. Part of the lower edge — of variable length — is straight or slightly concave; the posterior edge is produced to a rounded and often long, beak-like point. Young specimens are elongate and the upper and lower edge of the shell are almost parallel. The anterior part of the shell is rounded, the posterior part relatively pointed. As distinct from *Unio* species, the hinge is toothless. Like all members of the Unionidae family, the Swan Mussel varies markedly with the environment, which influences the shape and the size of the valves. In muddy to sandy fast-flowing water and in muddy stagnant or sluggish water they are quite different; their shape and size also depend on the amount of calcium and nutrients in the water and on many other factors. Consequently, the shape of the valves alters with changes in the environment and sometimes even in the course of an individual lifetime. This led in the past to the description of many species (about 400) which are today considered to be synonyms of a single species, i. e. *Anodonta cygnea*.
Colouring: brownish green, with a bluish green lustre inside. Inside the valves is mother-of-pearl.
Size: length 95—200 mm, height 60—120 mm, breadth 30—60 mm.
Habitat: mainly muddy stagnant or sluggish water (large fishponds, pools, creeks, large swamps).
Distribution: most European countries and Siberia.

2. *Pseudoanodonta complanata* ROSSMÄSSLER, 1835, **Compressed River Mussel** — European. The valves are smaller than in *A. cygnea*, are a broad oval or oval and only slightly swollen, so that the breadth of the shell (across the two valves) is barely half its height. The umbones are flatly convex; the sculpture on their anterior surface is faint or indistinct and consists of rounded and elongate tubercles. The anterior part of the shell is strikingly lower than the posterior part. The upper edge curves gently up to the escutcheon, which is low and has a bluntly rounded corner. From here the posterior edge slopes obliquely backwards in an almost straight line. The lower edge is usually regularly convex throughout and together with the posterior edge it forms, at the back, a blunt tip pointing slightly downwards. The posterior of the shell is about four times longer than the anterior. A very variable species.
Colouring: the periostracum has green and brown accretion bands.
Size: length 70—80 mm, height 40—45 mm, breadth 20 mm.
Habitat: large, quietly flowing rivers and sometimes large streams and lakes.
Distribution: central Europe from the Elbe in the east to the Weser in the west; to Finland and Sweden in the north. The related *P. elongata* inhabits Atlantic western Europe as far as the river Weser in Germany.

Family: **Sphaeriidae — Orb Mussels ('Pea Cockles')**

This widespread family contains viviparous and generally small bivalves with a flat-sided foot which can be extruded a long way out of the shell. The species belong mainly to the genera *Sphaerium* and *Pisidium*. The latter, which include the smallest species, generally inhabit shallow water or swamps with rotting vegetation, as well as rivers, canals and lakes.

The shells are mostly thin-walled and may have a grooved or ribbed surface. The hinge, which is visible only with the aid of a powerful magnifying glass, is important for their determination. The hinge plate is narrow and curved. Radiating out from the umbone are cardinal teeth, present in each valve. The lateral teeth are situated parallel to the hinge plate on either side of the umbo.

1. *Sphaerium rivicola* (LAMARCK, 1818), **Nut Orb Mussel** — central-east European. The shell is relatively thick-walled, strong, glossy, ovally elliptical and tumid. Sculpture on the umbo is almost smooth, but gradually becomes increasingly strongly ridged concentrically. The widely convex umbones are not very prominent above the hinge line; they are situated almost in the middle and tend to lean forwards. The valves are fairly symmetrical and the anterior part of the shell is a little lower and shorter than the posterior part. The lunule and the escutcheon are very low, but distinct; the ligament is exposed and is slightly prominent.
Colouring: the periostracum is dark reddish, yellowish or olive brown; the marginal zone is generally yellowish.
Size: relatively constant. Length 18—24 mm, height 15—18 mm, breadth 10—14 mm.
Habitat: a common species in all types of stagnant or sluggish water at low altitudes, it preferably frequents a muddy bed near the bank.
Distribution: from France, across central and eastern Europe, to the Ural basin, southwards to the middle and lower reaches of the Danube basin and northwards to England.

2. *Sphaerium solidum* NORMAND, 1844 — central-east European. The shell is relatively thick-walled, glossy and conspicuously and almost regularly concentrically grooved; it is thickest on the convexities and thinner round the edges. The umbone is widely convex and projects beyond the upper edge; it is manifestly inclined forwards and is sometimes abraded. The anterior part of the shell is slightly shorter than the posterior part and has a regularly rounded edge. The rounded edge of the posterior part terminates in a point; the escutcheon is faintly prominent. The ligament lies in a depression, but is clearly visible.
Colouring: the periostracum is light brown or yellowish grey.
Size: length 9—12 mm, height 8—9.5 mm, breadth 5.2—6.4 mm.
Habitat: sand in large rivers, generally in the current.
Distribution: France, Belgium, the Netherlands, Germany, Poland, the former USSR.

Family: **Sphaeriidae** — Orb Mussels ('Pea Cockles')

1. *Sphaerium corneum* (LINNAEUS, 1758), **Horny Orb Mussel** — Palaearctic. The valves are thin-walled, broadly oval and markedly tumid. Their surface is irregularly grooved with very faint radial lines and has a silky sheen. The umbones are wide, fully convex and rather low; they project very slightly above the upper edge, lie almost in the middle and are faintly inclined forwards. The very small lunule and escutcheon are indistinct; the ligament is embedded between the valves and is externally almost invisible. This highly variable species is strongly influenced by its environment. Its shape, the reciprocal ratio of its dimensions, its size, the thickness of its walls, the demarcation of the embryonic valves, the colouring of the shell and the hinge are the most subject to change.
Colouring: various shades of greyish brown, often with yellow bands.
Size: length 10—13 mm, height 8—10 mm, breadth 6—8 mm.
Habitat: one of the commonest molluscs in various types of stagnant and gently flowing water (rivers, creeks, dams, brooks, mill streams, swamps, fishponds). In some types of polluted water it forms layers literally several centimetres thick.
Distribution: most European countries, North Africa, Transcaucasia, the steppes east of the river Ural and Siberia as far as the Lena basin.

2. *Sphaerium lacustre* (MÜLLER, 1774), **Lake Orb Mussel** — Palaearctic. The shell is strikingly thin-walled, fragile and translucent, with roughly trapezoid contours and rounded corners; laterally it is compressed and fairly flat. Its surface is very finely and irregularly grooved and it has a silky sheen. The valves are symmetrical, the umbones are almost in the middle; they are slim and conspicuously prominent above the hinge line, with small, very sharply defined embryonic valves, which are inclined forwards and are known as umbonal caps. The lunule and the escutcheon are narrow and elevated like keels, with blunt, rounded corners. The upper edge is almost horizontal. The practically straight anterior edge slopes down fairly abruptly from the lunular corner and together with the markedly raised lower edge it forms an anteriorly rounded, but very distinct angle. The posterior edge slopes down very abruptly and, in a wide arc, joins the faintly elevated lower edge, which is convex and gently curved.
Colouring: greyish white or yellowish white, often with darker bands and a very light-coloured edge.
Size: has several forms varying as regards their shape and size. Length 8—10 mm, height 7—8 mm, breadth 4—4.5 mm.
Habitat: muddy stagnant and sluggish water (chiefly in lowlands), overgrown pools and creeks, quiet parts of rivers, swamps, lakes, fishponds, ditches and small periodic pools.
Distribution: most European countries, North Africa, the Caucasus region and northern Asia.

Pisidium amnicum (MÜLLER, 1774). See p. 198.

1

2

Family: **Dreissenidae**

The body structure, development and mode of life of the species of this family are clearly indicative of their kinship with marine bivalves. Their development is characterized by metamorphosis. First comes the egg, then a free-swimming, ciliated larva, which, after a time, develops into a sessile adult bivalve held in place by a byssus thread. This relatively small family is represented in Europe by only one genus, with just a few species. Otherwise it is distributed in western Africa and in Central and North America.

Dreissena polymorpha (PALLAS, 1771), **Zebra Mussel** — Pontic. The shell is triangularly boat-shaped, relatively thick-walled, strong, opaque and in young specimens fairly glossy. In the umbonal area the growth lines are fine, while towards the edge they are more irregular, coarse and rough. The umbo is formed directly from the anterior upper edge of the shell and projects forwards like a pyramid. From the upper and posterior edge the convexity of the valves increases abruptly forwards and upwards and culminates in a strikingly defined ridge or keel running in a gentle curve from the umbo to the other end of the valve and separating the almost flat anterior surface from the remaining, convex part of the valve. The ligament is externally barely visible. The hinge has neither teeth nor plates, except for the ridges bordering the ligamental furrow.

Colouring: the ground colour of the older parts of the shell is yellowish grey, with dark brown arcuate and zigzag lines and stripes; in young specimens the rough parts are usually dark brown.

Size: length 25—40 mm, height 13—18 mm, breadth 16—23 mm.

Habitat: large rivers and their arms, lakes and brackish water, where the mussels settle on both stones and moving objects (e. g. boats, rafts and the shells of other bivalves). It also establishes in underground ducts and water pipes.

Distribution: this bivalve originally inhabited rivers in the region of the Black Sea and the Caspian Sea. In the 19th century it was carried — mainly by ships and by birds — to large areas of central and western Europe. Lately it has appeared in a number of dams. It has spread in Britain through the canal system.

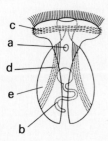

Larva of *Dreissena polymorpha*
a — mouth, b — intestine, c — cilia, d — muscles, e — embryonic valves.

Additional species living in the British Isles

Family: **Physidae** (p. 58)

Physa fontinalis (LINNAEUS, 1758), **Bladder Snail** — Holarctic. This sinistral shell resembles *P. acuta* (p. 58) but has a smaller and less elevate spire.
Size of shell: height 9—12 mm, width 6—8 mm, the aperture is three quarters of the height of the shell.
Habitat: common on weed in well oxygenated rivers, streams and canals in both soft and hard water.
Distribution: Holarctic — Europe and North America.

Family: **Lymnaeidae** (p. 60)

Lymnaea truncatula (MÜLLER, 1774), **Dwarf Pond Snail** — Holarctic. This dextral shell resembles *L. palustris* in shape (p. 62) but is smaller, paler brown with deeper sutures and more tumid whorls.
Colour: horn-coloured.
Size of shell: height 8—12 mm, width 4—6 mm. The aperture is a third of the height of the shell.
Habitat: in shallow waters of ditches, streams, small temporary pools, cart-ruts, often on acid ground with soft water. Amphibious and will remain inactive in mud during drought. Important as the intermediate host of the liver fluke *Fasciola hepatica*, a parasite of sheep and cattle.
Distribution: Holarctic — Europe and North America.

Family: **Planorbidae** (p. 64)

Bathyomphalus contortus (LINNAEUS, 1758), **Twisted Ramshorn** — Holarctic. Shell discoid and tightly coiled with 7—8 whorls which expand slowly. It is a chunky shell and taller in proportion to its width than many other planorbids. The aperture is crescent shaped.
Colour: yellow-brown, but often coloured darkly by deposits in the mud and also darkened in life by the colour of the animal showing through.
Size of the shell: a small shell, height 1.7—2 mm, width 5—6 mm.

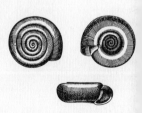

Habitat: often among weed in flowing and still waters of rivers, canals and lakes.
Distribution: throughout Europe to Siberia.

Gyraulus albus (MÜLLER, 1774), **White Ramshorn** — Holarctic. Shell discoid but fairly loosely coiled with only 4—4¹/₂ whorls, expanding increasingly rapidly to the aperture. Mouth and whorls fairly rounded, without a keel. The main diagnostic feature of this species is the distinct spiral sculpture on the shell seen through a hand lens.

Colour: typically white, but often darkened by external deposits from the mud.
Size of shell: one of the smaller planorbids, height 1.3—1.8 mm, width 4—7 mm.
Habitat: in most types of fresh water, among weed and on bottom mud, often in relatively poorly oxygenated water and not requiring a high level of calcium. Canals, rivers, ponds and lakes.

Hippeutis complanatus(LINNAEUS, 1758) (= *Segmentina complanata*), **Flat Ramshorn** — Palaearctic. A delicate, thin-walled, glossy shell which is very flat and lens-shaped with a distinct peripheral keel on the body whorl. The 3—4 whorls increase rapidly, so the shell is loosely coiled and the body whorl forms a considerable portion of the total area.

Colour: pale horn-coloured.
Size of shell: small, height 1—1.2 mm, width 2—3 mm.
Habitat: usually in still water of ponds, lakes and ditches with a fairly high level of calcium.
Distribution: Europe.

Family: **Chondrinidae** (p. 70)

Abida secale (DRAPARNAUD, 1801), **Large Chrysalis Snail** — Palaearctic. An elongate conical shell, taller than it is broad, with a pointed top consisting of 9—10 whorls, the pointed spire making up two thirds of the total height. The whorls are convex, separated by distinct sutures and expanding gradually. The mouth has a brownish-white lip and many tooth folds (8—9) in the aperture. The surface of the shell is matt, sculptured by axial growth lines.

Colour: brown or grey-brown.
Size of shell: height 6—8 mm, width 2.5—3 mm.
Habitat: lives on rocky hillsides in limestone areas.
Distribution: mostly western Europe, throughout

France, Switzerland, Austria, the Czech Republic, Slovakia, Germany, Belgium and the southern parts of the British Isles.

Family: **Vertiginidae** (p. 70)

Vertigo pusilla Müller, 1774, **Wall Whorl Snail.** Shell sinistral, elongate but narrowing both at the apex and at the aperture, with the widest part above the mouth. The 5 tumid whorls expand fairly rapidly and are separated by deep sutures which indent the profile of the spire. The aperture has a lip and six teeth in the mouth and there is a small umbilical cleft alongside. Shell surface glossy.
Colour: pale yellow-brown to white.
Size of shell: height 2 mm, width 1 mm.
Habitat: amongst moss and other vegetation on old walls, dry banks and mature sand-dunes.
Distribution: widespread throughout Europe.

Family: **Pupillidae** (p. 72)

Lauria cylindracea (DA COSTA, 1778), **Chrysalis Snail.** Shell dextral and barrel-shaped with a blunt apex, made up of 7 whorls which expand gradually; the body whorl takes up half of the total height. The shell is relatively thin, translucent and with a smooth glossy surface. The mouth has a peristome lip and a single white tooth on the parietal (upper) wall of the aperture.
Colour: usually brown, white specimens occasionally occur.
Size of shell: small, height 3.5—4 mm, width 1.8 —2 mm.
Habitat: in woods, under hedges and on walls, either at the base or under ivy or other plant cappings. Particularly common by the sea on cliff-top grassland.
Distribution: western Europe, throughout the British Isles and France with scattered localities in Norway and Sweden, Denmark and Germany.

Leiostyla anglica (WOOD, 1828) (= *Lauria anglica*), **English Chrysalis Snail.** Shell dextral with a more oval and conical spire compared with *Lauria cylindracea*, giving the shell a smoother outline. 6—7 whorls, separated by shallow sutures. When placed on a flat surface the shell rolls around very readily due to its shape. The mouth has a peristome lip and four teeth inside, distinguishing it from *L. cylindracea* along with the stronger axial growth lines.

190

Colour: horn-coloured, occasionally white.
Size of shell: height 3.75 mm, width 2 mm.
Habitat: woods, hedges and walls in damp places, particularly in areas of high rainfall, can be found in leaf litter.
Distribution: British Isles, throughout Ireland, Scotland, Wales and the west country, an isolated population in Sussex, but only sporadic occurrences on the Continent.

Family: **Valloniidae** (p. 72)

Vallonia costata (MÜLLER, 1774), **Ribbed Grass Snail.** Shell flattish, almost circular in outline with a round lip that has a conspicuous white peristome. The shell consists of only 3—4 whorls which expand gradually: underneath is a large open umbilicus. Similar in shape to *V. pulchella* (illustrated p. 72), but *V. costata* is distinguished by the conspicuous and widely spaced axial ribs.
Colour: white, but appearing cream-coloured when alive or fresh.
Size of shell: height 1.2—1.3 mm, width 2.3 —2.7 mm.
Habitat: amongst rock rubble, old walls, grass in fairly dry situations.
Distribution: virtually throughout Europe, except in northern Scotland and northern Scandinavia.

Acanthinula aculeata (MÜLLER, 1774), **Prickly Snail.** A small conical shell that is distinguished by the well spaced axial ribs which are raised into spines on the peripheral line.
Colour: brown.
Size of shell: height 2 mm, width 2 mm.
Habitat: in woodland and scrub, most usually found by sorting leaf litter.
Distribution: widespread in Europe except the more northern parts of Scandinavia.

Family: **Enidae** (p. 74)

Ena obscura (MÜLLER, 1774), **Lesser Bulin.** Shell similar to *E. montana* illustrated (p. 74) but smaller.
Size of shell: height 8—11 mm, width 3.5—4.5 mm.
Habitat: in woods and hedgerows: it can be found crawling on tree trunks in wet weather.
Distribution: throughout most of Europe with the ex-

ception of the northern parts of the British Isles and northern Scandinavia.

Family: **Succineidae** (p. 78)

Catinella arenaria (BOUCHARD-CHANTEREAUX, 1837), **Sand-bowl Amber Snail.** A dextral conical-ovate shell with well expanded body whorl. *C. arenaria* is closest in shape to *Succinea oblonga,* which also has deep sutures and a taller spire but differs from the other species illustrated (p. 79) in the smaller aperture, less swollen body whorl as well as the deep sutures and taller spire.
Colour: amber.
Size of shell: the smallest in the family. Height 4.5—6 mm, width 3—3.6 mm.
Habitat: wet hollows or slacks in sand-dune systems.
Distribution: a rare snail with a limited range in the British Isles (Ireland and North Devon) where it is a protected species under the Wildlife and Countryside Act. Elsewhere in northern Scandinavia with scattered but isolated populations in other countries.

Succinea oblonga (DRAPARNAUD, 1801), **Small Amber Snail.** Shell similar to *C. arenaria* but a little larger with slightly less prominent sutures.
Colour: yellow to amber.
Size of shell: height 6—10 mm, width 3—5 mm.
Habitat: marshes and along ditches.
Distribution: widespread on the Continent of Europe, but a rare snail of only local occurrence in the British Isles (Ireland and Scotland) and small areas of Norway and Sweden.

Family: **Arionidae** (p. 82)

Arion hortensis agg., **The Garden Slug.** This former aggregate species has now been sub-divided into three:
Arion distinctus MABILLE, 1868, which is blue-black and has the tip of the tail the same colour. (Picture see p. 86)
A. hortensis FÉRUSSAC, 1819, also blue-black but with an orange tip to the tail.
A. owenii DAVIES, 1979, brownish dorsal surface, tentacles pinkish, tip of tail with dark and light stripes.
These slugs are difficult to identify in the field and a group of species which needs to be confirmed by dissection of the reproductive system.

Geomalacus maculosus (ALLMAN, 1843), **Kerry Slug** — Atlantic. A spectacular slug with a spotted body of dark grey and white with smooth tubercles. The breathing pore opens near the anterior end of the mantle shield, showing relationship with the arionid slugs. There is an oval shell plate inside the mantle. Size: extends to about 70 mm.
Habitat: in damp places under moss; it rolls up like a woodlouse when disturbed.
Distribution: a rare slug with a very restricted range in the wetter oceanic climate of S. W. Ireland, Brittany and N. W. Spain.

Family: **Vitrinidae** (p. 88)

Phenacolimax major (FÉRUSSAC, 1807), **Greater Pellucid Glass Snail.** Shell rather similar to the more common *Vitrina pellucida* illustrated (p. 88) but the animal of *Phenacolimax major* is black rather than grey and quite distinctive.
Colour: shell a yellowish green.
Shell size: height 3.5 mm, width 5—6 mm.
Habitat: old woodlands.
Distribution: western Europe: southern Britain, France, Belgium, the Netherlands, Germany and parts of Switzerland.

Family: **Zonitidae** (p. 90)

Aegopinella nitidula (DRAPARNAUD, 1805), **Waxy Glass Snail.** Very similar to *A. nitens* illustrated (p. 91), but the two species have a different distribution. *A. nitidula* is found in northwestern Europe in a wide variety of habitats.

Aegopinella pura (ALDER, 1830), **Clear Glass Snail.** Like a miniature *A. nitidula* or *A. nitens,* but with a white shell.
Shell size: height 2—2.6 mm, width 4—4.5 mm.
Habitat: moist places including woodland leaflitter and wet grassland.
Distribution: throughout most of Europe.

Oxychilus cellarius (MÜLLER, 1774), **Cellar Glass Snail.** Shell flat and glossy with a narrow umbilicus typical of the genus. This species differs from *O. draparnaudi* (illustrated p. 93) in its flatter spire, pale yellow or cream shell, pale grey body and in the more even expansion of the body whorl which does not expand or

drop suddenly at the lip and in the double lines of the sutures.

Size of shell: height 5—5.5 mm, width 10—11 mm.

Habitat: a wide range of habitats from woodland to gardens.

Distribution: most of Europe except the far east and northern Scandinavia.

Oxychilus alliarius (MILLER, 1822), **Garlic Snail**. This species is distinguished by its more open umbilicus, smaller size (6 mm) and particularly by the strong smell of garlic emitted when the animal is prodded.

Habitat: woodland and grassy places, often common on acid soil.

Distribution: north-western Europe: the British Isles, Belgium, Netherlands, Germany, Denmark, Poland, southern Scandinavia and possibly France.

Oxychilus helveticus (BLUM, 1881), **Glossy Glass Snail**. Shell discoidal, thin, transparent, highly glossy with a very narrow umbilicus. Only a slight smell of garlic.

Shell size: height 5 mm; breadth 8—10 mm.

Colour: rich brown. In the animal there is a distinct black edge to the mantle in this species.

Habitat: damp places such as woods and among rocks and stones.

Distribution: north-west Europe including Britain. Continental distribution not fully known.

Nesovitrea hammonis (STRÖM, 1765), **Rayed Glass Snail**. Flat and glossy, but fairly loosely coiled with a wide umbilicus. Distinguished by widely spaced rayed axial grooves on the dorsal or top surface of the shell.

Size of shell: height 2—2.5 mm, width 3.5—4.5 mm.

Habitat: damp places including woodland (leaf litter), marshes and wet grassland.

Distribution: throughout Europe.

Zonitoides excavatus (ALDER, 1830), **Hollowed Glass Snail**. Shell flat and shiny, many whorls and tightly coiled. There is a large umbilicus which is very wide.

Colour: brown or greenish brown.

Size of shell: height 3 mm, width 6—7 mm.

Habitat: woodland and sometimes grassland, always on acid soil (a calcifuge).

Distribution: throughout the British Isles, the Netherlands, Germany and Denmark.

Family: **Milacidae** (p. 100)

Tandonia sowerbyi (FÉRUSSAC, 1823), (= *Milax sower-byi*), **Sowerby's Slug** — Atlantic. Like *T. budapestensis* (illustrated p. 101) there is a dorsal keel from tail to mantle shield that is paler than the body. *T. sowerbyi* is distinguished by its larger size (up to 80 mm), a pale rim round the breathing pore and a uniformly pale cream foot sole.
Habitat: common in gardens and disturbed places.
Distribution: British Isles and western France.

Family: **Limacidae** (p. 94)

Limax flavus (LINNAEUS, 1758), **Yellow Slug**. A yellow mottled body with blue-grey tentacles.
Size: extended 70—95 mm.
Habitat: typically around human settlements, gardens, cellars and old walls; active only after dark and spends daytime hidden deeply in crevices.
Distribution: western and central Europe.

Limax maculatus (KALENICZENKO, 1851) (= *L. grossui* LUPU, 1970; *L. pseudoflavus* EVANS, 1978), **Green Slug**. Similar in shape and size to *L. flavus*, but has a more greenish body, rougher tubercles and also differs in details of the reproductive system.
Size: 70—95 mm.
Habitat: under logs and rocks in woodlands.
Distribution: not fully known; throughout Ireland and a few sites in the rest of the British Isles, Romania and former USSR.

Family: **Agriolimacidae** (p. 100)

Deroceras caruanae POLLONERA, 1891. Similar to *D. reticulatum* (illustrated p. 101) in size and shape but differs in being a uniform dark pinky-brown with a white rim to the breathing pore.
Size: 25—20 mm.
Habitats: grassy places but more frequently on agricultural land, gardens and waste places.
Distribution: not fully known, as this slug has changed its range much in the last 20 years. British Isles, Mediterranean. The true nomenclature and identity of this slug is in some doubt and liable to change.

Deroceras laeve (MÜLLER, 1774), **Marsh Slug**. A small

version of *D. caruanae* that lacks the white rim round
the breathing pore as well as differences in the repro-
ductive system.
Size: 17—25 mm.
Habitat: marshes.
Distribution: throughout Europe.

Family: **Boettgerillidae** (p. 100)

Boettgerilla pallens SIMROTH, 1912. A curious worm-
like slug with a keel from tail to mantle shield.
Size: 30—40 mm.
Habitat: in woods in eastern Europe, but parks and
gardens elsewhere.
Distribution: eastern Europe, but also introduced to
the west and found in several scattered localities in
Britain.

Family: **Clausiliidae** (p. 102)

Clausilia bidentata (STRÖM, 1765), **Two-toothed Door
Snail.** Shell sinistral, spindle-shaped and narrower in
relation to its width than many other species in the
family. The whorls are sculptured by well-formed axial ribs.
Colour: variable — dark reddish-brown to beige.
Shell size: height 13 mm, width 2.5 mm.
Habitat: tree trunks and logs in woods, under the
shelter of ivy or basal vegetation of old walls and in
rock rubble.
Distribution: in most countries of western Europe.

Family: **Helicidae** (122)

Candidula intersecta (POIRET, 1891) (= *Helicella capera-
ta* MONTAGU), **Wrinkled Snail.** Shell of similar shape
and texture to *Candidula unifasciata*, illustrated p.
129, but shell distinguished by its stronger and less
regular axial ribs.
Shell size: height 8 mm, width 12 mm.
Colour: chalky white ground colour with variable
brown markings.
Distribution: western Europe: British Isles, France,
Belgium, Netherlands, Denmark and some localities
in western Germany.

Candidula gigaxii (PFEIFFER, 1850) (= *Helicella gigaxii*), **Eccentric Snail.** Shell similar to *C. intersecta* but

distinguished by finer and neater axial ribbing and a more eccentric umbilicus.

Habitat: Grassland. Often on roadsides and verges on calcareous soil.

Distribution: western Europe: France. Britain, Belgium and parts of the Netherlands.

Monacha cantiana (MONTAGU, 1803) (= *M. cemenelea* RISSO), **Kentish Snail**. A sub-globular shell, whitish in colour but with part of the body whorl suffused with red. The body whorl is more globular than in *Trichia striolata*.

Size: height 14 mm, width 14—20 mm.

Habitat: an open country species of fields, downs and grassy roadsides.

Distribution: north-west Europe in Britain, France, Belgium, Netherlands and western part of Germany, but in the larger form (*cemenelea*) in Italy and the south of France.

Monacha granulata (ALDER, 1830) (= *Ashfordia granulata*), **Silky Snail**. Endemic to Britain. Shell dextral, sub-globular but rather conical with an elevate spire and a broad base. The thin shell is densely hairy and this species is distinguished from other hairy snails by the white colour of the shell and the minute umbilicus (separating it from *Trichia hispida*) and by the shell shape and taller spire (separating it from young *Monacha cantiana*).

Colour: white shell.

Shell size: height 5.5 mm, width 8 mm.

Habitat: in damp places, but restricted to marshy ground in S. E. England, while it occurs also in hedgerows in the south-west.

Distribution: endemic to the British Isles and Ireland and localities are well scattered.

Zenobiella subrufescens (MILLER, 1822), **Dusky Snail** or **Brown Snail**. Noted for its exceptionally thin brown shell which is little calcified and bends. Sub-globular in shape with well developed body whorl (slightly keeled in juveniles) and well marked sutures. The umbilicus underneath is minute.

Shell size: height 6 mm; width 10 mm.

Colour: chestnut brown.

Habitat: amongst tufts of grass and herbs in woodlands and shady places.

Distribution: western Oceanic, biased towards the western half of Britain and Ireland and along the Atlantic coast of France.

Ponentina subvirescens (BELLAMY, 1839) (= *Hygromia revelata*), **Green Hairy Snail**. Shell globular, rather thin and with periostracal hairs, particularly in juveniles. A rather deep suture and small umbilicus.
Shell size: height 4—5 mm; breadth 5—7 mm.
Colour: greenish yellow.
Habitat: at bases of rocky outcrops on sea cliffs and on stone walls by the coast.
Distribution: western Europe: Spain, Portugal, western France and the south-west of the British Isles and Channel Islands.

Class: **Bivalvia**
Family: **Sphaeriidae** (182)

Pisidium amnicum (MÜLLER, 1774), **Large Pea Shell**. The largest and easiest species of *Pisidium* to identify. A white to cream-coloured asymmetrical shell with distinctive concentric ribbing parallel with the ventral margin.
Size: length 8—11 mm; height 5—8.5 mm.
Habitat: in fine sand or mud of calcareous rivers, streams and canals.
Distribution: generally distributed throughout Europe.

Key for the identification of European mollusc families

(Living specimens are required to work this key)

Class: Gastropoda
1. Operculum on the dorsal surface of the back of the foot which closes the aperture when the animal withdraws into the shell . . . . Subclass Prosobranchia . . 2.
— Without an operculum . . . . Subclass Pulmonata . . . . 10.
2. Hemispherical shell with a straight-surfaced aperture, very thick walls and 2—3 whorls (the last one strongly dominant). Aquatic . . . . Family **Neritidae**.
— Shape of shell variable, the last whorl less strongly dominant and its width normally not more than half the width of the shell . . . . 3.
3. Animal a land gastropod . . . . 4.
— Animal an aquatic gastropod with gills . . . . 7.

4. Shell small (less than 4.5 mm), generally smooth, tall and cylindrical, highly glossy and unicoloured . . . . Family **Aciculidae.**
— Shell larger (over 5 mm) and sculptured . . . . 5.
5. Shell narrowly conical and normally finely grooved, with 8—10 whorls, and 6—15 mm tall . . . . Family **Cyclophoridae.**
— Shell with a reticular structure and larger than the preceding shells . . . . 6.
6. Shell is broadly conical, with 4—5 whorls, and is 13—20 mm high. Spiral sculpture . . . . Family **Pomatiasidae.**
— Size, colouring and shape of the shell variable and the whorls mostly convex to highly dilated . . . . 7.
7. Shell large (usually over 25 mm high), conically ovoid, with three brownish longitudinal bands on the whorls . . . . Family **Viviparidae**
— Shell generally unicoloured, bandless and moderately large to small (generally less than 20 mm high) . . . . 8.
8. Shell slimly conical and sharp-pointed, with 8—9 whorls and no umbilicus; height 15—25 mm. The aperture is narrowly oval . . . . Family **Thiaridae.**
— Shell smaller (less than 15 mm) and differently shaped . . . . 9.
9. Shell up to 7 mm, conically spherical, flatly conical or discoid, with a narrow to very wide umbilicus and tightly spiral operculum . . . . Family **Valvatidae.**
— Height of shell always greater than its width, aperture is not circular and the whorls the same height as (or higher than) the aperture (except in the genus *Lithoglyphus)* . . . . Family **Hydrobiidae.**
10. Land snail has two pairs of retractile tentacles on its head, with the eyes at the end of the upper pair. . . . . Order Stylommatophora . . . . 15.
— Largely aquatic snail with one pair of non-retractile tentacles, with eyes at their base . . . . Order Basommatophora . . . . 11.
11. Shell has no whorls and is cap- or boat-shaped; tip is inclined backwards and twisted sideways . . . . Families **Ancylidae** and **Acroloxidae.** (Freshwater limpets)
— Shell spirally coiled . . . . 12.
12. Shell measures about 2 mm, is conical, with three teeth in the aperture. Inhabits damp places . . . . Family **Ellobiidae**
— Shell always larger than 2 mm, with a simple, toothless aperture . . . . 13.
13. Shell discoid; the whorls are sunken or level with one another. . . . . Family **Planorbidae.**
— Spire elevate . . . . 14.
14. Shell dextral, tentacles triangular . . . . Family **Lymnaeidae.**
— Shell sinistral, thin-walled and highly glossy, tentacles slender and filiform . . . . Family **Physidae.**
15. Gastropod without an external shell; breathing pore on the right side, at the edge of the mantle . . . . Slugs . . . . 16.
— Gastropod with a shell . . . . Snails . . . . 17.
16. Breathing pore in the anterior half of the mantle. The back is rounded and without a keel . . . . Family **Arionidae.**
— Breathing pore in the posterior half of the mantle shield. A sharp keel runs along the mid dorsal line from the tail — its extent varying with the family . . . . Families **Milacidae, Limacidae, Agriolimacidae**.
17. Shell dextral and variably shaped . . . . 19.
— Shell mainly sinistral and is ovoid or fusiform . . . . 18.

18. Shell fusiform (spindle-shaped) and at least 7 mm high . . . . Family **Clausiliidae.**
— Shell minute (not more than 3 mm high), elliptical or ovoid . . . . Family **Vertiginidae.**
19. Shell thin-walled and transparent, with a sharp, straight-edged aperture; width always exceeds height and the last whorl is strikingly dominant. The animal is generally unable to withdraw into its shell . . . . Families **Vitrinidae, Testacellidae.**
— Shape and size of the shell vary; if the last whorl widens, its width never exceeds 2/5 of the width of the shell . . . . 20.
20. Height of the shell markedly exceeding its width . . . . 21.
— Shell wider than it is high, or the two dimensions are approximately the same . . . . 25.
21. Aperture margin is simple and sharp, no umbilicus, shell roundly ovoid, slimly conical or awl-shaped . . . . 22.
— Aperture margin is thick and wide, often with folds or other protuberances, and the shell is differently formed . . . . 23.
22. Shell slender to conically ovoid, with up to four whorls, the last moderately or strongly dominant; usually amber-coloured . . . . Family **Succineidae.**
— Shell is awl-shaped, slimly conical or cylindrical, colourless or light-coloured, with 3—6 whorls; 5—50 mm high . . . . Families **Ferussaciidae, Oleacinidae, Subulinidae.**
23. Shell highly lustrous, translucent and almost smooth, 4—7 mm; toothless aperture has a thick lip . . . . Family **Cochlicopidae.**
— Shell opaque, umbilicus very narrow and the closed or concealed aperture generally armed with teeth . . . . 24.
24. Shell relatively large, elongate and conically or cylindrically ovoid. Aperture either toothless or with three large teeth . . . . Family **Enidae.**
— Shell measures less than 10 mm and is roundly ovoid, conical or claviform; aperture is usually armed with teeth . . . . Families **Pupillidae, Orculidae, Chondrinidae.**
25. Shell very flat and convexly discoid, umbilicus very wide, edge of the aperture sharp and upper surface ribbed; width 1.5—8 mm . . . . Family **Endodontidae.**
— Shell variable; forms with a wide umbilicus are distinguished by a widened or everted margin, generally with a lip or a smooth surface . . . . 26.
26. Shell 2.5—5 mm wide and variously formed, with a wide umbilicus . . . . Families **Pyramidulidae, Valloniidae.**
— Shell large, medium sized or small; small forms have no umbilicus, but a sharpedged aperture . . . . 27.
27. Shell is mainly small to moderately large and thin-walled, with or without an umbilicus, and highly transparent and always unicoloured; the margin is straight and sharp, surface faintly grooved or smooth. Shell compressed and rounded, or is spherically conical . . . . Families **Zonitidae, Euconulidae.**
— Shell moderately large to large, umbilicus generally open and often wide, walls relatively thick and aperture margin usually everted with a lip. Shell generally spherical or slightly compressed and rounded; width 5—60 mm 28
28. Shell spherical, about 18 mm across, umbilicus open and moderately wide aperture margin wide and sharp-edged, with a very flat lip. Colour: greyish

white to light reddish brown and transparent, sometimes with a brown band round the periphery . . . . Family **Bradybaenidae.**
— Shell different; species similar in form and size are distinguishable by their narrow, concealed umbilicus or by their different surface structure . . . . 29.
29. Shell spherical, moderately large, thick-walled, smooth and chalk-white, with closed umbilicus and 5—6 whorls . . . . Family **Sphincterochilidae.**
— Shell differently coloured . . . . 30.
30. Shell small to large, often thick. The shape varies from discoidal through subglobular to globular. Juveniles are often slightly keeled. The shell lip is often thickened and reflected. The surface is only heavily sculptured in some genera while others exhibit periostracal hairs . . . . . . Family **Helicidae**

Class: Bivalvia

1. Valves triangularly carinate, with the umbones nearer the anterior end of the upper margin. Sessile adult animals are attached to various objects in the water . . . . Family **Dreissenidae.**
— Valves are differently formed, but length is their dominant dimension . . . . 2.
2. Valves large and in adult specimens do not measure less than 50 mm. The umbones lie a long way anteriorly and the hinge is either toothless or has large teeth . . . . Families **Unionidae, Margaritiferidae.**
— Valves small or minute, hinge equipped with fine teeth and umbones situated posteriorly or almost in the middle . . . . Family **Sphaeriidae.**

Key for the identification of British terrestrial species

This key mostly relies on features of the shell, but it works best with fresh specimens since long dead shells become weathered and can loose their identification characters. Although experienced conchologists can name them, worn shells are best avoided by the beginner.

When a snail is alive the colour and markings of the animal can show through the shell if it is not completely opaque, thus altering the overall colour. When the animal is prodded with a pencil point, it will retreat further into the shell, allowing the shell colour to be assessed at the lip.

One of the main problems met by the beginner to the study of snails is that of identifying juveniles. Snails are prolific breeders and up to 75 percent of a population of one species may be immature. This key attempts to accommodate the problem of juveniles, some species being in the key in more than one position. Juvenile helicids are often detected by a slight peripheral keel which is lost or reduced in the adult, and in these the spire is flatter in young than in mature specimens. Another clue is the size of the protoconch or embryo shell at the apex. Large snails generally lay large eggs and in these the protoconch is also larger — compare the apices of *Helix aspersa* and *Monacha cantiana*. The size of the protoconch is used in separating *Aegopinella nitidula* and *A. pura*, although the latter is often recognised by its white shell.

In some species, e. g. *Cepaea*, the shell colour varies considerably, but in others, e. g. *Trichia hispida* it is fairly constant. Occasionally albino shells occur.

The easiest way of separating the species of *Cepaea* is by the colour of the lip, but occasionally there are genetic variants in which brown lips are found in specimens of *C. hortensis* and white lips in *C. nemoralis*. Abnormal size is normally the indication of change in lip colour.

The key may not work with excessively worn shells or unusual variants, but it should work with the majority of species. Some sketches are included in the key and the reader is advised to refer also to line drawings and photographs in the main text of the book.

In some situations, like the difficult Amber Snails (Succineidae) and the Whorl Snails *(Vertigo)*, the key does not go down to species. Readers are then advised, having arrived at the genus, or a selection of species, to work through the descriptions in the text for the final identification.

Key to British land snails

1. Shell taller than broad, height/breadth ratio at least 3:2 (use ruler to check)   2

1. Shell globular or flat with diameter equal to or greater than height 30

2. Shell 5 mm or more in height   3
2. Shell less than 5 mm in height 20
3. Shell thick with spiral sculpture dominant. Operculum closing mouth in live specimen . . . . . *Pomatias elegans* (Round-mouthed Snail)
3. Sculpture or ribbing not as above   4
4. Shell spindle-shaped with marked longitudinal (axial) ridges or ribs which are more distinct and regular than growth lines (lens)   5
4. Shell comparatively smooth   6
5. Shell breadth 2.5 mm or less, height of adult about 10 mm. Spindle-shaped, sinistral with teeth in mouth of shell in adult (use lens). Common on walls, rocks and in woodland. *Clausilia bidentata* (Two-toothed Door Snail)
5. Shell breadth more than 2.5 mm, adult 11—18 mm in height. Not glossy. *Clausilia dubia* (Craven Door Snail): north of England, *Macrogastra rolphii* (Rolph's Door Snail): south-east England and the Midlands

operculum

Laciniaria biplicata (Two-lipped Door Snail): limited distribution in Thames valley

6. Teeth in mouth of adult shell   7

6. Shell without teeth in the mouth 11

7. Found on the shore, rocks, caves or salt-marsh turf   8
7. Not in marine situations   9
8. Shell brown, living in salt-marsh turf and mud. *Ovatella myosotis* (Mouse-ear-shelled Snail)
8. Shell whitish, under stones of brackish lagoons or rocky shore. *Leucophytia bidentata* (Two-toothed White Snail)
9. Shell with mouth on left (sinistral), spindle-shaped, polished and up to 18 mm in height. Occurs in woodland . . . *Cochlodina laminata* (Plaited Door Snail)

9. Shell with mouth on right (dextral) 10
0. Shell solid, matt surface and with many teeth in the mouth of adult shell. Found on limestone or chalk grassland . . . . *Abida secale* (Large Chrysalis Snail)

0. Shell thin and glossy with narrow constricted mouth and usually three teeth. Sutures very shallow . . . *Azeca goodalli* (Three-toothed Snail)

1. Found on salt-marshes, saline lagoons or rocky shores (juveniles)   8
1. Not as above 12
2. Shell consisting of a large swollen body whorl with only a small spire. Amphibious . . . . Amber Snails (Succineidae)
. . . . 13

12. Shell tall and comparatively narrow with well formed spire. Body whorl not so greatly swollen ....,...... 13

13. Fresh specimen with glossy shell 14
13. Fresh specimen with dull shell 18
14. Exceptionally shallow sutures between whorls ...
.... 15
14. Moderate sutures. Shell usually brown, broad protoconch 16
15. Shell white, straight-sided, less than 6 mm. Animal white and without eyes, living in soil........... *Cecilioides acicula* (Blind Snail)

15. Shell usually brown, broader and triangular-shaped. Animal with eyes at tips of tentacles ..... *Azeca goodalli* (Three-toothed Snail) juvenile
16. Shell with mouth on right (dextral) .... *Cochlicopa lubrica* and *C. lubricella* (Slippery Moss Snails)
16. Shell with mouth on left (sinistral) 17
17. Shell fairly parallel-sided with blunt apex .... *Cochlodina laminata* (Plaited Door Snail) juvenile
17. Shell somewhat triangular with whorls of graded sizes. Up to 9 mm in height ...... *Balea perversa* (Tree Snail), (see p. 119)
18. Shell opaque, white with variable brown markings. Tumid whorls. Height to 25 mm. Sand-dunes by the sea .... *Cochlicella acuta* (Pointed Snail)
18. Shell uniform brown or pinkish 19

19. Found on dry limestone grassland in the south ... *Abida secale* (Large Chrysalis Snail) juvenile or weathered shell of *Cochlicopa lubrica* (Slippery Moss Snail)

19. Found in woods or hedgebanks, no teeth in the mouth ...... *Ena obscura* (Lesser Bulin) 8—11 mm high or *E. montana* (Bulin) 12—18 mm high
20. Shell white in live examples 21
20. Shell brownish........................ 22

21. Shell with pointed apex, a tall triangular spire, teeth in mouth of adult shell. Height 2 mm. Animal white with eyes at base of tentacles. Found in leaf litter of woods and marshes . . . . . . *Carychium tridentatum* (Long-toothed Herald Snail) in woods or *C. minimum* (Short-toothed Herald Snail) in marshes

21. Shell with blunt apex, straight-sided, mouth narrow and without teeth. Lives underground. Animal white without eyes . . . . . *Cecilioides acicula* (Blind Snail)

22. Shell uniformly slender, 3 × 1 mm, glossy, usually brown with well spaced axial sculpture. Operculum in live examples. Moist logs and leaf litter . . . . *Acicula fusca* (Point Snail)

22. Not as above 23

23. Shell with one or more teeth in the mouth . . . 24

23. Shell without teeth in the mouth 28

24. Adult shell with only one apertural tooth on top lip 25

24. Adult shell with more than one tooth in mouth 26

25. Body whorl occupying less than half the height of shell. Barrel-shaped, pale mauvy brown, matt surface and white fleck on body whorl behind lip. Found on calcareous grassland and dunes . . . . *Pupilla muscorum* (Moss Snail)

25. Body whorl occupying half of the height of the shell. Barrel-shaped, brown and polished surface. Found on walls, logs, trees and waysides by the sea
. . . . *Lauria cylindracea* (Chrysalis Snail)

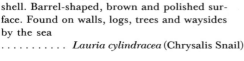

26. Shell with mouth on the left (sinistral) 27

26. Shell with mouth on the right (dextral)
.... 7 species of *Vertigo* (Whorl Snails)
and *Leiostyla anglica* (English Chrysalis Snail)

27. Found on walls, dunes and banks ....
.... *Vertigo pusilla* (Wall Whorl Snail)
27. Found in marshes .... *Vertigo angustior* (Narrow-mouthed Whorl Snail)
28. Shell with mouth lip reflected in adult ......
Columella edentula or *C. aspera* (Toothless
Chrysalis Snail)
28. Shell lip not thickened or finished off 29
29. Shell highly glossy in live specimens, large
apex or protoconch
... *Cochlicopa lubrica* agg. (Slippery Moss
Snail) juveniles
29. Shell barrel-shaped with smaller protoconch ... juveniles of *Lauria*, *Pupilla*, *Leiostyla*, *Columella* and *Vertigo* species.
30. Shell triangular, globular or subglobular with
little difference between height and diameter. 31

30. Shell flat, or with the spire only slightly
raised. Diameter distinctly greater than
height 52

31. Shell diameter more than 10 mm 32
31. Shell diameter less than 10 mm 37
32. Shell more than 30 mm across 33
32. Shell less than 30 mm across 34
33. Shell thick, very large protoconch, indistinct
outer varnish layer. South of England, mostly
North Downs ...... *Helix pomatia* (Roman
Snail)
33. Distinct varnish layer to shell, blotched pattern. Gardens, disturbed ground and sand
dunes ...... *Helix aspersa* (Common Garden
Snail)
34. Shell completely yellow or pink, with or
without up to five brown spiral bands. Surface
usually polished 35
34. Not as above, possibly with whitish flecks on
maroon shell 36
35. Lip of adult shell brown, diameter up to
25 mm ... *Cepaea nemoralis* (Brown-lipped Snail)

35. Lip of adult shell white, diameter up to 20 mm . . . . *Cepaea hortensis* (White-lipped Snail)

36. Shell usually brown-maroon with dark peripheral band and white flecks, especially on underside. Body usually dark . . .
. . . *Arianta arbustorum* (Orchard Snail)

36. Not as above 37

37. Shell with distinct hairs on surface (use lens) . 38

37. Shell surface without hairs (use lens) 42

38. Shell greenish. Found on cliffs in the southwest . . . .
. . . . . . *Ponentina subvirescens* (Green Hairy Snail)

38. Not as above 39

39. Shell with comparatively large body whorl, shell whitish and fairly small umbilicus . . . .
. . . . . . *Monacha cantiana* (Kentish Snail) juvenile

39. Shell more coiled 40

40. Shell with few hairs, somewhat keeled at periphery, colour variable . . . .
. . . . . *Trichia striolata* (Strawberry Snail) juvenile

40. Not as above 41

41. Shell brown, umbilicus fairly open. Shell to 8 mm . . . .
. . . . . *Trichia hispida* (Hairy Snail) and *T. plebeia* (smaller umbilicus)

41. Shell whitish, rather conical with very small umbilicus . . . .
. . . . . *Monacha granulata* (Ashford's Hairy Snail)

42. Shell surface with radial ribbing (use lens) . . . 43

42. Shell surface with growth lines only 46

43. Shell triangular with flat base and keel. Introductions in southeast only . . . .
. . . . *Trochoidea elegans* (Top Snail)

43. Not as above, more globular 44

44. Shell white and chalky with variable brown markings, umbilicus present . . . .
. . . *Candidula intersecta* (Wrinkled Snail) and *C. gigaxii* (Eccentric Snail)

44. Shell brownish and small (to 2.5 mm) 45

45. Ribs widely spaced with spines at periphery . . . . .
. . . . *Acanthinula aculeata* (Prickly Snail)

45. Ribs closer together and without spines . . .
        . . . *Spermodea lamellata* (Plaited Snail)

46. Shell consisting almost entirely of body whorl . . .
        . . . 47

46. Shell with several whorls and spire 48

47. Shell oval in outline, often greenish, translu-
cent . . . .

        . . . . *Vitrina pellucida* (Pellucid Glass
Snail), *Phenacolimax major* (Greater Pellucid
Glass Snail), *Semilimax pyrenaica* (Pyrenean
Glass Snail)

47. Shell circular in outline with comparatively
large protoconch . . . .
        . . . . juveniles of *Cepaea, Arianta* and *Helix*

48. Shell thin and translucent, brown, minute um-
bilicus 49

48. Not as above 50

49. Shell with flat base, up to 3 mm . . . .
    . . . *Euconulus fulvus* and *E. alderi* (Tawny
Glass Snails)

49. Shell more globular, up to 9.5 mm . . . .
    . . . . *Zenobiella subrufescens* (Dusky or
Brown Snail)

50. Shell with very small umbilicus . . . .
    . . . . *Monacha cartusiana* (Carthusian
Snail), *Hygromia cinctella* (Girdled Snail), *H.
limbata* (Hedge Snail)

50. Shell with distinct umbilicus, especially in
adult 51

51. Shell thick and chalky, whitish with variable
brown pattern . . . .
    . . . . *Theba pisana* (Sandhill Snail), south-
west only, *Cernuella virgata* (Banded Snail)

51. Shell not so thick . . .
        . . . *Monacha cantiana* (Kentish Snail), *Trichia
striolata* (Strawberry Snail)

52. Shell diameter more than 5 mm 53

52. Shell diameter less than 5 mm 62

53. Shell thin, translucent, smooth and often glossy, never with thickened lip. (Live or freshly
dead shells necessary) 54

53. Shell opaque and not highly glossy. Some
have thickened lips and a rib inside the
mouth when adult 58

208

54. Umbilicus narrow, shell highly glossy . . .
      . . . *Oxychilus* (Glass Snails) 4 species

54. Umbilicus (hole underneath) large and loosely
    coiled, shell matt or glossy 55

55. Shell of many whorls, large open umbilicus
    (hole underneath) 57

55. Shell with comparatively few whorls, less
    tightly coiled 56

56. Shell with slight peripheral keel . . . . ju-
    venile Helicids 37

56. Shell with no keel, waxy surface . . .
      . . . *Aegopinella nitidula* (Waxy Glass Snail)

57. Shell rich brown, animal black with orange
    spot on mantle. Found on marshy ground . . . . . .
    . . . . *Zonitoides nitidus* (Shiny Glass Snail)

57. Shell greenish in colour, smooth and glossy.
    Acid woods and grassland . . . .
    . . . . . *Zonitoides excavatus* (Hollowed Glass Snail)

58. Umbilicus (hole underneath) large and open
    (a quarter width of shell or more) 59

58. Umbilicus smaller than above 61

59. Shell with distinct axial ribbing and often red
    wedges on body whorl, shell tightly coiled . . .
      . . . *Discus rotundatus* (Rounded Snail)

59. Shell surface smooth 60

60. Shell brownish, shaped like a round disc. Ju-
    veniles hairy. Old woodland . . . .
    . . . . *Helicodonta obvoluta* (Cheese Snail)

60. Shell whitish, usually with brown markings
    and bands. Up to 20 mm. Calcareous soils on
    downs and dunes . . *Helicella itala* (Heath Snail)

61. Shell thick, with strong peripheral keel.
    Brownish. On rocks, walls and tree trunks . . . . . .
    . . . . *Helicigona lapicida* (Lapidary Snail)

61. Shell without a keel (or only slight one in ju-
    veniles) 62

62. Shell white and chalky with brown markings
and axial ribbing or strong growth lines . . . .
. . . . *Candidula intersecta* (Wrinkled Snail)
C. gigaxii (Eccentric Snail), *Cernuella virgata*
(Banded Snail) juvenile
62. Shell brown when fresh, smooth and without
pattern 63
63. Spire completely flat, no keel . . .
. . . *Helicodonta obvoluta* (Cheese Snail)
63. Spire somewhat raised and with a slight keel . 64
64. Shell with hairs or hair pits (use lens), pale
brown. Adult diameter to 7 mm . . . .
. . . . *Trichia hispida* (Hairy Snail)
64. Shell usually without hairs, colour variable
but with pale peripheral line. Adult diameter
to 13 mm . . . . *Trichia striolata* (Strawberry Snail)

65. Shell white or cream with rounded and thickened trumpet-like mouth in adult. Umbilicus
large. Juveniles recognised by large umbilicus, matt surface and deep sutures. Up to
2.5 mm (use lens) 66
65. Without thickened lip 67
66. Shell with widely spaced axial ribs (use lens) . . .
. . . *Vallonia costata* (Ribbed Grass Snail)

66. Shell smooth . . . .
. . . . *Vallonia excentrica* (Eccentric Grass
Snail) on dry grassland, *V. pulchella* (Smooth
Grass Snail) on wet grassland
67. Shell translucent, smooth, glossy with well
spaced radiating grooves (use hand lens), usual-
ly brown. Up to 5 mm . . .
. . . *Nesovitrea hammonis* (Rayed Glass Snail)

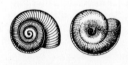

67. Shell not as above 68
68. Shell brown 69
68. Shell white 73
69. Shell with axial ribbing . . . .
. . . . . . *Candidula intersecta* (Wrinkled Snail),
C. gigaxii (Eccentric Snail), *Discus rotundatus*
(Rounded Snail)

69. Shell without ribs or peripheral keel 70
70. Shell with small, narrow umbilicus . . .
. . . *Oxychilus* spp. (Glass Snails) juveniles
70. Shell with more open umbilicus 71
71. Adult shell very small (2 mm), tightly coiled . . .
. . . *Punctum pygmaeum* (Pygmy Snail)

71. Shell more than 2 mm across 72
72. Shell thin, rather flat, a dull shine, adult up to
    8 mm . . . .
    . . . . *Aegopinella nitidula* (Waxy Glass Snail)

72. Shell thicker and opaque, shaped like a cheese.
    Adult up to 15 mm . . . .
    . . . . *Helicodonta obvoluta* (Cheese Snail)
73. Umbilicus very small, shell glossy . . .
    . . . *Vitrea* spp. (Crystal Snails)
73. Umbilicus more open 74
74. Shell up to 2 mm, glossy, tightly coiled. Lives
    in soil. Animal blind and without eye spots . . .
    . . . *Helicodiscus singleyanus*
74. Shell up to 4 mm, less tightly coiled, matt sur-
    face . . . . *Aegopinella pura* (Clear Glass Snail)

Bibliography and societies

An atlas has been published showing the distribution of non-marine molluscs in the British Isles on a 10 km square grid (Kerney 1976). There are three societies in Britain concerned with the study of molluscs of which the Conchological Society of Great Britain and Ireland is the one most active in field work and was involved in the production of the atlas. Addresses of the societies are given below:

The Conchological Society of Great Britain and Ireland
For amateurs and professionals. Holds lecture and field meetings and publishes a journal and a newsletter.
Details from: Mrs. E. B. Rands, 51 Wychwood Avenue, Luton, Bedfordshire LU2 7HT.

The Malacological Society of London
Mostly for professionals but amateurs welcome. Holds meetings and symposia and publishes a journal and bulletin.
Hon. Secretary: Dr. J. A. Crame, British Antarctic Survey, High Cross, Madingley Road, Cambridge CB3 6ET

British Shell Collectors' Club
Primarily for amateurs. Holds a shell show and annual convention and publishes a newsletter.
Hon. Secretary: Mr. Kevin Brown, 12 Grainger Road, Isleworth, Middlesex TW7 6PQ

References

CAMERON, R. A. D., EVERSHAM, B. and JACKSON, N., 1983. A field key to the slugs of the British Isles. *Field Studies* 5, 807—824.

CAMERON, R. A. D. and REDFERN, M., 1976. British land snails. *Synopses of the British Fauna* (New Series) No. 6. The Linnean Society of London, Academic Press, London.

CLESSIN, S., 1987. Molluskenfauna Österreich-Ungarns und der Schweiz. 858 pp., Nürnberg.

DAMYANOV, S. G., LIKHAREV, I. M., 1975. Fauna Bulgarica, 4. Gastropoda terrestria. 423 pp., Sofia.

EHRMANN, P., 1956. Mollusca. *Die Tierwelt Mitteleuropas*, II/1, 264 pp., Leipzig.

EVANS, J. G., 1972. Land snails in archaeology. Seminar Press, London.

FRETTER, V. and GRAHAM, A., 1962. British Prosobranch Molluscs. Ray Society, London.

FRETTER, V. and PEAKE, J. (editors), 1978. Pulmonates. Vol. 2A, Systematics, Evolution and Ecology. 540 pp., Academic Press, London.

GITTENBERGER, E., 1973. Beiträge zur Kenntnis der Pupillacea, III. Chondrininae. Zoologische Verhandlungen, 127, 267 pp., Leyden.

GROSSU, A. V., 1955, 1962. *Fauna Republicii Populare Romine*. Mollusca, III/1 — Gastropoda Pulmonata, 518 pp., III/3 — Bivalvia, 426 pp., Bucharest.

JANUS, H., 1982. The Illustrated Guide to Molluscs. Harold Starke, London.

JANUS, H., 1968. Unsere Schnecken und Muscheln. Kosmos Naturführer, 124 pp., Stuttgart.

KERNEY, M. P., 1976. Atlas of the Non-marine Mollusca of the British Isles. Conchological Society of Great Britain and Ireland and Natural Environment Research Council, Huntingdon.

KERNEY, M. P., 1976. A list of the fresh and brackish-water mollusca of the British Isles. *Journal of Conchology* 29, 26—28. London.

KERNEY, M. P., CAMERON, R. A. D., 1979. A Field Guide to the Land Snails of Britain and North-west Europe. 288 pp., Collins, London.

KERNEY, M. P., CAMERON, R. A. D. and JUNGBLUTH, J. H., 1983. Die Landschnecken Nord- und Mitteleuropas. Paul Parey, Hamburg and Berlin.

KLEMM, W., 1974. Die Verbreitung der rezenten Land-Gehäuse-Schnecken in Österreich. Denkschriften der Österreichischen Akademie der Wissenschaften, 117, 502 pp., Springer, Vienna, New York.

LIKHAREV, I. M. and RAMMELMEIER, E. S., 1952. Land Mollusc Fauna of the USSR (in Russian). 511 pp., Moscow, Leningrad.

LIKHAREV, I. M., VIKTOR, A., 1980. The slug fauna of the USSR and adjacent countries (Gastropoda terrestria nuda). Fauna USSR, III/5, 437 pp., Leningrad.

LOŽEK, V., 1956. A Key to Czechoslovak Molluscs. 437 pp., Bratislava (in Czech).

LOŽEK, V., 1973. Nature in the Quaternary Era. 372 pp., Academia, Prague (in Czech).

LOŽEK, V., 1964. Quartärmollusken der Tschechoslowakei, Rozpravy Ústředního ústavu geologického, Vol. 31, 374 pp., Prague.

MACAN, T. T., 1960. A key to the British fresh- and brackish-water gastropods. Scientific Publication No. 13. Freshwater Biological Association, Ambleside, Cumbria.

PINTER, L., RICHNOVSZKY, A. and SZIGETHY, A. S., 1979. Distribution of the Recent Mollusca of Hungary. *Soosiana* Supplement 1.

ROSSMÄSSLER, E. A., 1835—1859. Iconographie der Land- und Süsswasser-Mollusken, Dresden, Leipzig.

SHILEIKO, A. A., 1978: Land molluscs of the superfamily Helicoidea. *Fauna SSSR* (Mollyuski), III/6, 360 pp., Leningrad (in Russian).

WALDEN, H. W., 1976. A nomenclatural list of the land mollusca of the British Isles. *Journal of Conchology* 29, 21—25.

WENZ, W. and ZILCH, A., 1959—1960. Handbuch der Paläozoologie, VI/2, Gastropoda Euthyneura, 834 pp., Berlin.

ZHADIN, V. I., 1952. Freshwater and Salt Water Molluscs of the USSR, 376 pp., Moscow, Leningrad (in Russian).

ZILCH, A. and JAECKEL, S. G. A., 1962. *Die Tierwelt Mitteleuropas*, Mollusken, II/1 — Ergänzungen. 294 pp., Leipzig.

INDEX

Figures in italics refer to illustrations.